Pennard Road Pro~ ~il
McPherson for the ~~~~
presents

EVENTS WHILE GUARDING THE BOFORS GUN

by John McGrath

FINBOROUGH | THEATRE

First performance at the Finborough Theatre: Tuesday, 22 May 2012

First published by Methuen & Co. Ltd. In 1966. Then by fairplay press, an imprint of Capercaillie Books Limited in 2009.
This theatre edition is published by Capercaillie Books in 2012.
Registered office 1 Rutland Court, Edinburgh.

Printed in the UK by CPI Group (UK) Ltd, Croydon, CR0 4YY
A catalogue record for this book is available from the British Library.
ISBN 978-1-906220-77-8

John McGrath

Cast in alphabetical order

Gunner O'Rourke	**Charles Aitken**
Lance-Bombardier Evans	**Lee Armstrong**
Gunner Flynn	**Phil Cheadle**
Gunner Rowe	**Michael Shelford**
Gunner Crawley	**Mark Stanley**
Second Lieutenant Pickering / Cook–Private Samuel / German	**Greg Tannahill**
Gunner Shone	**Samuel Taylor**
Sergeant Walker	**Anthony Topham**
Gunner Featherstone	**Alex Warren**

The action takes place in West Germany, 1954.

The performance lasts approximately two hours and fifteen minutes.

There will be one interval of fifteen minutes.

Director	**Robert Hastie**
Designer	**James Perkins**
Lighting Designer	**Nicholas Holdridge**
Composer	**Michael Bruce**
Sound Designer	**Tom Meehan**
Costume Designer	**Sophia Simensky**
Assistant Director	**George Ransley**
Dialect Coach	**Maeve Diamond**
Production Manager	**David Leigh-Pemberton**
Stage Manager	**Sophie Goody**
Assistant Stage Manager	**Sophie Sierra**
Casting Director	**Ava Morgan**
Press Representative	**Kate Morley**
Production Photographer	**Graham Michael**
Producers	**Caroline Dyott and Leonora Twynam**

Our patrons are respectfully reminded that, in this intimate theatre, any noise such as rustling programmes, talking or the ringing of mobile phones may distract the actors and your fellow audience-members.

We regret there is no admittance or re-admittance to the auditorium whilst the performance is in progress.

Charles Aitken | Gunner O'Rourke
Trained at RADA.
Theatre includes *Little Eagles* (Royal Shakespeare Company and Hampstead Theatre), *King Lear, As You Like It, Antony and Cleopatra* (Royal Shakespeare Company and Roundhouse), *The Drunks* (Royal Shakespeare Company), *Othello* (Frantic Assembly and Lyric Hammersmith – nominated for an Ian Charleson Award), *The Taming Of The Shrew* (Wiltons Music Hall), *Midnight Cowboy* (Assembly Rooms, Edinburgh), *Paradise Lost* (Oxford Stage Company), *Hair* (Gate Theatre, London) and *London Assurance* (Royal Exchange Theatre, Manchester).
Film and Television includes *Bonkers, The Girl On The Train* and *Love Nest*.

Lee Armstrong | Lance-Bombardier Evans
Trained at East 15 Acting School.
Theatre includes *The Europeans, The Rose and the Ring, A Winter's Tale, Three Sisters, A View from a Bridge* (East 15).
Lee is also a member of the National Youth Theatre.

Phil Cheadle | Gunner Flynn
Trained at RADA.
Theatre includes *Neighbourhood Watch, Dear Uncle* (Stephen Joseph Theatre, Scarborough), *Bedlam, Henry IV Parts 1 and 2* (Shakespeare's Globe), *Knives and Hens, Tartuffe* (Arcola Theatre), *All My Sons* (Curve Theatre, Leicester), *Mrs Affleck* (National Theatre), *Far From the Madding Crowd* (English Touring Theatre), *If I Were You* (Library Theatre, Manchester), *The Tempest, Saint Joan* (AndBC Theatre Tour), *Macbeth* (West Yorkshire Playhouse), *The Changeling* (Cheek by Jowl), *A Midsummer's Night Dream* (Creation Theatre), *Strawberry Fields* (Pentabus) and *As You Like It* (Northcott Theatre, Exeter).
Film includes *John Carter of Mars, Comes a Bright Day* and *A Touch of Sadness*.
Television includes *Inside the Titanic, Coronation Street* and *Inspector Lynley*.

Michael Shelford | Gunner Rowe
Trained at Bristol Old Vic Theatre School.
Theatre includes *The Boy On The Swing* (Arcola Theatre), *The Daughter-In-Law* (New Vic, Newcastle-under-Lyme), *On The Razzle, Romeo and Juliet* (Bristol Old Vic), *Gizmo Love* (Alma Tavern Theatre, Bristol), *Days Of Significance, Three Sisters, The Importance of Being Earnest* (Bristol Old Vic Theatre School) and *Aladdin* (Redgrave Theatre, Bristol).
Television includes *Lewis* and *Mrs Briggs*.
Radio includes *Smiley's People, The Archers, Ruminations, Slaughterhouse 5*. Michael was a member of the BBC Radio Repertory Company from 2009 to 2010. He was a runner up for the BBC Carleton Hobbs Radio Drama Prize and a Spotlight Prize Nominee 2009.

Mark Stanley | Gunner Crawley
Trained at the Guildhall School of Music and Drama.
Theatre includes '*Tis a Pity She's a Whore* (West Yorkshire Playhouse), *Still Life, Six Characters Looking for an Author, A Midsummer Night's Dream, Tipping the Velvet, Hamlet, The Trojan Women, The Relapse, One For the Road* and *The Three Sisters* (Guildhall School of Music and Drama).
Film includes *Captain America*.
Television includes *Game of Thrones* and the forthcoming *Air Aces*.

Greg Tannahill | Second Lieutenant Pickering / Cook – Private Samuel / German
Trained at LAMDA.
Theatre includes *Cabaret, Arcadia, Dancing At Lughnasa, Our Country's Good, A Gloriously Mucky Business, As You Like It, Some Voices, The Cherry Orchard, The Double Dealer, The Merchant of Venice* (LAMDA), *The Shoemaker's Holiday* (Sam Wanamaker Festival for LAMDA and Shakespeare's Globe), *Irons* (Local Girl Productions) and *The Possibilities, Two Gentlemen Of Verona* (Year Out Drama).
Film includes *Skeletons Warming Themselves*.

Samuel Taylor | Gunner Shone
Trained at LAMDA.
Theatre includes *The Art Of Persuasion, 50 Years New, The Girl Who Lost Her Voice, 40 Years On* (Stephen Joseph Theatre, Scarborough), *As You Like It, The Merchant of Venice* (The Lamb Players), *The Talented Mr Ripley, Redemption Over Hammersmith Broadway, A Woman Of No Importance, The Last Days Of Judas Iscariot, Scenes From An Execution* (LAMDA), *Beachy Head, Mile End* (Analogue) and *Macbeth* (Lakeside Arts Centre, Nottingham).
Radio includes *Life Begins At Crawley*.
Television includes *Holby City*.

Anthony Topham | Sergeant Walker
Theatre includes *Rhinestone Mondays* (UK Tour), *Look Back in* Anger (Eastern European première, Slovenia), *Mamma Mia!* (Prince of Wales), *The Rocky Horror Picture Show* (European tour) and *A Slice of Saturday Night* (King's Head Theatre).
Film includes *Soul Mate, Operation Chastity, The Silence, London Town* and *Claude's Room*.
Television includes *Casualty, Relative Strangers* and *Whodunnit*.

Alex Warren | Gunner Featherstone
Trained at LAMDA.
Theatre includes *Hamlet* (Shakespeare's Globe and National Tour), *Mad Forest* (BAC), *The Odyssey* (National Theatre), *Twelfth Night* (LAMDA) and *20 Cigarettes* (National Youth Theatre).
Film includes *Kissing And..., 7 Lives* and *From Nowhere*.
Television includes *Holby City, Being Human* and *Aces Falling*.

John McGrath | Playwright

John McGrath (1935-2002) was a prolific writer best known for his work with the 7:84 Theatre Company and for his extraordinary commitment to the importance of popular theatre. Born in Liverpool and raised in Wales, his writing career began at the BBC. He continued to work in television and film throughout his career including writing the screenplays for the films *Billion Dollar Brain* (1967) and *The Bofors Gun* (1968), but his chief passion was for the theatre. In 1971 he founded 7:84 Theatre Company, dedicated to taking popular, political theatre far and wide, particularly to towns and villages usually considered to be off the cultural map, and often presenting plays specially written for the company by McGrath. His plays include *Random Happenings in the Hebrides* (1970), *The Cheviot, The Stag and the Black, Black Oil* (1973, and subsequently televised), *The Game's A Bogey* (1974), *Little Red Hen* (1975), *Yobbo Nowt* (1975), *Out of Our Heads* (1976), *Blood Red Roses* (1980), *Mairi Mhor* (1985, and subsequently televised), *Border Warfare* (1989), *Watching for Dolphins* (1992) and *Hyperlynx* (2001). John McGrath died in 2002. Playwright Trevor Griffiths wrote in his obituary: "while his life may be over, I get the feeling his work is just beginning."

Robert Hastie | Director

Trained as an actor at RADA.

Directing includes *The Middle Man*, *In The Land of Uz*, *A Lost Expression*, *David and Goliath*, *Snow in Sheffield* (Bush Theatre), *This Modern Man* (The Miniaturists at the Arcola), and as co-director *The Merchant of Venice* and *As You Like It* (The Lamb Players).

Theatre as Associate Director includes *Sixty-Six Books* (Bush Theatre), *Much Ado About Nothing* (Wyndham's Theatre) and as Assistant Director *2:18 Underground* (National Youth Theatre).

James Perkins | Set Designer

At the Finborough Theatre, James designed *Trying* (2009) and *Foxfinder* (2011).

James is one third of theatre collective paper/scissors/stone, resident designer for Charles Court Opera and a member of Forward Theatre Project.

Other theatre includes *Floyd Collins* (Southwark Playhouse), *The Girl in The Yellow Dress* (Salisbury Playhouse), *The Fantasist's Waltz* (Theatre Royal York), *Matters of Life and Death* (National Tour), *Many Moons* (Theatre 503), *Beowulf* (Charles Court Opera), *Stockwell* (Tricycle Theatre), *The Marriage of Figaro* (Wilton's Music Hall), *Saraband* (Jermyn Street Theatre), *Girls and Dolls*, *Colourings* (Old Red Lion Theatre), *Iolanthe*, *Through The Woods* (Pleasance, London), *The Pirates of Penzance*, *HMS Pinafore* (Buxton Opera House), *The Barber* (Greenwich Theatre) and *The Wonder* (BAC).

Forthcoming theatre includes *The Only True History of Lizzie Finn* (Southwark Playhouse), *St John's Night* (Jermyn Street Theatre) and *Lost in Yonkers* (Watford Palace Theatre).

Nicholas Holdridge | Lighting Designer

Theatre includes *Sense and Sensibility* (UK Tour), *Beowulf*, *The Panto* (Charles Court Opera), *Memory Cells*, *Scott Mills the Musical* (Pleasance Edinburgh), *Much Ado About Nothing*, *A Midsummer Night's Dream* (Mercury Theatre, Colchester), *Wink the Other Eye*, *Uncle Vanya* (Wilton's Music Hall) and *Immodesty Blaize and Walter's Burlesque!* (Arts Theatre).

Dance includes *The Firebird* (English National Ballet), *Silent Steps*, *Inside Out*, *RUSH*, *Duality* (Pair Dance) and *Spare Rib* (Scarlett Perdereau).

Opera includes *Xerxes*, *Don Giovanni* (Iford Arts), *The Yeomen of the Guard* (Buxton Opera House), *Edgar* (Feria de Valladolid) and *The Mikado*, *Trial by Jury* (Charles Court Opera).

Michael Bruce | Composer

Michael is Composer in Residence at the Donmar Warehouse. He was previously Resident Composer at the Bush Theatre and the recipient of the Notes for the Stage Prize for song writing.

Theatre includes *Noises Off* (Old Vic and Novello Theatre), *The Recruiting Officer*, *The Physicists* (Donmar Warehouse), *The 24 Hour Plays* (The Old Vic); *Sixty-Six Books* (Bush Theatre), *The Pied Piper and Musicians of Bremen* (Roundhouse), *Much Ado About Nothing* (Wyndham's Theatre), *Men Should Weep* (National Theatre), *Ed: The Musical* (Edinburgh Festival and Trafalgar Studios), *Michael Bruce at the Apollo* (Apollo Theatre), *The Great British Country Fete* (National Tour, Latitude Festival and Bush Theatre) and *Christmas in New York* (Lyric Theatre and Prince of Wales Theatre).

Orchestrations and arrangements include *Friday Night Is Music Night* (BBC Radio 2), *Ruthie Henshall in Concert* (The Guildhall, London) and *Helena Blackman: The Sound of Rodgers and Hammerstein* (Speckulation Entertainment).

Tom Meehan | Sound Designer
Trained at Mountview Academy of Theatre Arts.
Theatre includes *Aladdin* (Hertford Theatre), *About Bill* (Landor Theatre) and *Kiss* (White Bear Theatre). He was Assistant Sound Designer on *Sixty-Six Books* (Bush Theatre). Tom has also worked at venues including The Young Vic, Opera Holland Park, Leicester Square Theatre, The Cochrane Theatre, The Lowry Quays Theatre, The Manchester Opera House and Bernie Grant Arts Centre.
Theatre while training includes *On the Shore of The Wide World* (Jackson's Lane Arts Centre), *Rent*, *Carousel* (Bernie Grant Arts Centre) and *PG Directors Season* (Karamel Club).

Sophia Simensky | Costume Designer
At the Finborough Theatre, Sophia is Costume Designer for the forthcoming *An Incident at the Border* (2012).
Trained at the Wimbledon College of Art.
Other theatre includes *You and Me* (Rich Mix), *Oranges on the Brain* (Pegasus Theatre, Oxford), *Ink* (Chase the Crane Theatre Company) and *The Changeling* (Underbelly Edinburgh).
Film includes *Screaming Guns*.

George Ransley | Assistant Director
George is currently Resident Assistant Director at the Finborough Theatre where he assisted Phil Willmott on *The American Clock* (2012) and Veronica Quilligan on *Autumn Fire* (2012).
Previously, he assisted Blanche McIntyre on *Repentance* and *Behind the Lines* (Angle and Bush Theatre). Direction whilst studying includes *Rope*, *Rosmersholm*, *Housekeeping* – Theatre Uncut (Bedlam Theatre, Edinburgh) and *Amadeus* (Bedlam Theatre, Edinburgh, and The National Student Drama Festival 2011 where it was Winner of the Audience Award for Best Production, The Cameron Mackintosh Award for Best Use of Music, and The Spotlight Best Actor and Actress Awards), *Macbeth* (Edinburgh University Shakespeare Society Highland Tour), *Opera Sins* (Edinburgh Festival) and, as Assistant Director, *The Cunning Little Vixen* (Pleasance, Edinburgh).

Ava Morgan | Casting Director
Ava is Casting Assistant at Chloe Emmerson Casting, working on a range of theatre, film and commercials. *Events While Guarding the Bofors Gun* is Ava's first independent casting project. Recent Casting Assistant credits include *Fear*, *Chalet Lines* and *Our New Girl* (all Bush Theatre). Prior to this, Ava worked as a Publicist in Arts and Entertainment PR on projects as diverse as The Old Vic, Hackney Empire, Bush Theatre, the Kenwood Picnic Concerts, the British Military Tournament at Earl's Court, *Legally Blonde* on tour and the West End productions of *Wicked*, *Million Dollar Quartet* and *Clybourne Park*. Ava trained in Musical Theatre at the Arts Educational Schools, London, and spent three seasons with Festival Highlights at the Edinburgh Festival as a Production and PR Assistant.

Caroline Dyott | Producer
At the Finborough Theatre, Caroline produced *The Man* (2010) and its subsequent national tour. Caroline is currently Associate Producer at English Touring Theatre. Prior to this she worked at the Bush Theatre for four years, both as Producer and Head of Individual Giving. Freelance producing includes *The Unspeakable* (Tristan Bates Theatre) and *The 24 Hour Plays* (Old Vic New Voices). She is on the Advisory Board of non zero one, and last year completed the Clore Emerging Leaders Course.

Leonora Twynam | Producer
Leonora currently splits her time between freelance producing and working as a lawyer. She worked in the Development Department at the Bush Theatre for four years, was on the committee for *The 24 Hour Plays* (Old Vic New Voices) for seven years and continues to be a governor of Central School of Speech and Drama.

The Producers would like to thank the generous donors and supporters without whom this production would not have been possible: Anonymous, Sarah Cooke, Clyde Cooper, Victoria Gray, Alexander and Ika Green, Francois and Arrelle von Hurter, Neil LaBute, Georgia Oetker, Comte and Comtesse Patrick de Pelet, Peter Wilson.

The production is also indebted to the help and support of Edd Boughton of Fourfeet Design (www.fourfeet.co.uk), Peter Collins, Alastair Coomer, James Dowling (www.ukwatches.com), Mekel Edwards, Chloe Emmerson, English Touring Theatre, Tom Erhardt, Jack Gold, Barry Jackson, Blanche McIntyre, Elizabeth McLennan, Sabre Sales, The Shaftesbury Centre, Derek Spence, Michaela Stogden, The Tabernacle W11, Jon Trenchard and Terry Warren.

FINBOROUGH | THEATRE

Winner – Eight awards at the OffWestEnd Awards 2012

"A theatre in a class of its own: last year's programme was so good that it was worth moving to West Brompton for...Its first new writing premiere of the year...suggests that 2012 in London's only wine bar theatre, will be as impressive as it was in 2011." *Time Out*

"A disproportionately valuable component of the London theatre ecology. Its programme combines new writing and revivals, in selections intelligent and audacious." *Financial Times*

"A blazing beacon of intelligent endeavour, nurturing new writers while finding and reviving neglected curiosities from home and abroad." *The Daily Telegraph*

Founded in 1980, the multi-award-winning Finborough Theatre presents plays and music theatre, concentrated exclusively on new writing and genuine rediscoveries from the 19th and 20th centuries. We aim to offer a stimulating and inclusive programme, appealing to theatregoers of all ages and from a broad spectrum of the population. Behind the scenes, we continue to discover and develop a new generation of theatre makers – through our vibrant Literary team, our internship programme, our Resident Assistant Director Programme, and our partnership with the National Theatre Studio providing a bursary for Emerging Directors.

Despite remaining completely unsubsidised, the Finborough Theatre has an unparalleled track record of attracting the finest creative talent, as well as discovering new playwrights who go on to become leading voices in British theatre. Under Artistic Director Neil McPherson, it has discovered some of the UK's most exciting new playwrights including Laura Wade, James Graham, Mike Bartlett, Sarah Grochala, Jack Thorne, Simon Vinnicombe, Alexandra Wood, Al Smith, Nicholas de Jongh and Anders Lustgarten.

Artists working at the theatre in the 1980s included Clive Barker, Rory Bremner, Nica Burns, Kathy Burke, Ken Campbell, Jane Horrocks and Claire Dowie. In the 1990s, the Finborough Theatre became known for new writing including Naomi Wallace's first play *The War Boys*; Rachel Weisz in David Farr's *Neville Southall's Washbag*; four plays by Anthony Neilson including *Penetrator* and *The Censor*, both of which transferred to the Royal Court Theatre; and new plays by Richard Bean, Lucinda Coxon, David Eldridge, Tony Marchant, Mark Ravenhill and Phil Willmott. New writing development included a number of works that went to become modern classics including Mark Ravenhill's *Shopping and F***king*, Conor McPherson's *This Lime Tree Bower*, Naomi Wallace's *Slaughter City* and Martin McDonagh's *The Pillowman*.

Since 2000, new British plays have included Laura Wade's London debut *Young Emma*, commissioned for the Finborough Theatre; James Graham's *Albert's Boy* with Victor Spinetti; Sarah Grochala's *S27*; Peter Nichols' *Lingua Franca*, which transferred Off-Broadway; and West End transfers for Joy Wilkinson's *Fair*; Nicholas de Jongh's *Plague Over England*; and Jack Thorne's *Fanny and Faggot*. The late Miriam Karlin made her last stage appearance in *Many Roads to Paradise* in 2008. Many of the Finborough Theatre's new plays have been published and are on sale from our website.

UK premieres of foreign plays have included Brad Fraser's *Wolfboy*; Lanford Wilson's *Sympathetic Magic*; Larry Kramer's *The Destiny of Me*; Tennessee Williams' *Something Cloudy, Something Clear*; the English premiere of Robert McLellan's Scots language classic, *Jamie the Saxt*; and three West End transfers – Frank McGuinness' *Gates of Gold* with William Gaunt and John Bennett, Joe DiPietro's *F***ing Men* and Craig Higginson's *Dream of the Dog* with Dame Janet Suzman.

Rediscoveries of neglected work have included the first London revivals of Rolf Hochhuth's *Soldiers* and *The Representative*; both parts of Keith Dewhurst's *Lark Rise to Candleford*; *The Women's War*, an evening of original suffragette plays; *Etta Jenks* with Clarke Peters and Daniela Nardini; Noël Coward's first play, *The Rat Trap*; Charles Wood's *Jingo* with Susannah Harker; Emlyn Williams' *Accolade* with Aden Gillett and Graham Seed; and Lennox Robinson's *Drama at Inish* with Celia Imrie and Paul O'Grady.

Music Theatre has included the new (premieres from Grant Olding, Charles Miller, Michael John LaChuisa, Adam Guettel, Andrew Lippa and Adam Gwon's *Ordinary Days* which transferred to the West End) and the old (the UK premiere of Rodgers and Hammerstein's *State Fair* which also transferred to the West End, and the acclaimed Celebrating British Music Theatre series, reviving forgotten British musicals including *Gay's The Word* by Ivor Novello with Sophie-Louise Dann, Helena Blackman and Elizabeth Seal.

The Finborough Theatre won *The Stage* Fringe Theatre of the Year Award in 2011, won *London Theatre Reviews'* Empty Space Peter Brook Award in 2010, the Empty Space Peter Brook Award's Dan Crawford Pub Theatre Award in 2005 and 2008, the Empty Space Peter Brook Mark Marvin Award in 2004, four awards in the inaugural 2011 OffWestEnd Awards and swept the board with eight awards at the 2012 OffWestEnd Awards including Best Artistic Director and Best Director for the second year running. *Accolade* was named Best Fringe Show of 2011 by *Time Out*. It is the only unsubsidised theatre to be awarded the Pearson Playwriting Award bursary for writers Chris Lee in 2000, Laura Wade in 2005 for James Graham in 2006, for Al Smith in 2007, for Anders Lustgarten in 2009, Simon Vinnicombe in 2010 and Dawn King in 2011. Three bursary holders (Laura Wade, James Graham and Anders Lustgarten) have also won the Catherine Johnson Award for Pearson Best Play. **www.finboroughtheatre.co.uk**

FINBOROUGH | THEATRE

118 Finborough Road, London SW10 9ED
admin@finboroughtheatre.co.uk
www.finboroughtheatre.co.uk

Artistic Director | **Neil McPherson**
Resident Designer | Deputy Chief Executive | **Alex Marker**
General Manager | **Harriet Uff**
Assistant General Managers | **Lauren McGee, Isabella Riggs**
Pearson Playwright-in-Residence | **Dawn King**
Playwrights-in-Residence | **Bekah Brunstetter, James Graham, Anders Lustgarten, Colleen Murphy, Simon Vinnicombe**
Associate Director | **Justin Audibert**
Cameron Mackintosh Resident Composer facilitated by Mercury Musical Developments and Musical Theatre Network UK | **Craig Adams**
Literary Manager | **Francis Grin**
Literary Associate Music Theatre | **Max Pappenheim**
Senior Reader | **Aoife Moylan**
Technical Manager | **Miguel Figueiredo**
Associate Designer | **Philip Lindley**
Marketing | **Gemma Bealing**
Resident Casting Director | **Hayley Kaimakliotis**
Resident Assistant Director | **George Ransley**
and our many interns and volunteers
The General Manager position is supported by an anonymous donor

 The Associate Director position is supported by The National Theatre Studio's Bursary for Emerging Directors, a partnership between the National Theatre Studio and the Finborough Theatre.

 The Finborough Theatre has the support of the Pearson Playwrights' Scheme. Sponsored by Pearson PLC.

  The Cameron Mackintosh Resident Composer Scheme is facilitated by Mercury Musical Developments and Musical Theatre Matters

 STAGETEXT Captioned Performances
Captioning converts the spoken word into text that provides people with hearing loss with access to live performance.
www.stagetext.org

 The Finborough Theatre is a member of the Independent Theatre Council, Musical Theatre Network UK and The Earl's Court Society www.earlscourtsociety.org.u

  Ecovenue is a European Regional Development Fund backed three year initiative of The Theatres Trust, aiming to improve the environmental sustainability of 48 small to medium sized performing arts spaces across London.
www.ecovenue.org.uk

 The Finborough Wine Café
Contact Monique Ziervogel on 020 7373 0745 or finboroughwinecafe@gmail.com

Online

 www.facebook.com/FinboroughTheatre

 www.twitter.com/finborough.

Mailing

Email admin@finboroughtheatre.co.uk or give your details to our Box Office staff to join our free email list. If you would like to be sent a free season leaflet every three months, just include your postal address and postcode.

Feedback

We welcome your comments, complaints and suggestions. Write to Finborough Theatre, 118 Finborough Road, London SW10 9ED or email us at admin@finboroughtheatre.co.uk

Friends

The Finborough Theatre is a registered charity. We receive no public funding, and rely solely on the support of our audiences. Please do consider supporting us by becoming a member of our Friends of the Finborough Theatre scheme. There are four categories of Friends, each offering a wide range of benefits.
Brandon Thomas Friends – Bruce Cleave. Matthew Littleford. Sean W. Swalwell.
Richard Tauber Friends – Neil Dalrymple. M. Kramer. Harry MacAuslan. Brian Smith. Mike Lewendon. Lionel Monckton Friends – Bridget MacDougall.
William Terriss Friends – Leo and Janet Liebster. Peter Lobl. Bhags Sharma. Thurloe and Lyndhurst LLP. Jon Sedmak. Jan Topham.

Smoking is not permitted in the auditorium and the use of cameras and recording equipment is strictly prohibited.

In accordance with the requirements of the Royal Borough of Kensington and Chelsea:

1. The public may leave at the end of the performance by all doors and such doors must at that time be kept open.

2. All gangways, corridors, staircases and external passageways intended for exit shall be left entirely free from obstruction whether permanent or temporary.

3. Persons shall not be permitted to stand or sit in any of the gangways intercepting the seating or to sit in any of the other gangways.

The Finborough Theatre is licensed by the Royal Borough of Kensington and Chelsea to The Steam Industry, a registered charity and a company limited by guarantee. Registered in England no. 3448268. Registered Charity no. 1071304. Registered Office: 118 Finborough Road, London SW10 9ED. The Steam Industry is under the Artistic Direction of Phil Willmott. www.philwillmott.co.uk

Characters

LANCE-BOMBARDIER EVANS

GUNNER SHONE

GUNNER FLYNN

GUNNER CRAWLEY

GUNNER ROWE

GUNNER FEATHERSTONE

GUNNER O'ROURKE

SERGEANT WALKER

SECOND LIEUTENANT PICKERING

COOK, PRIVATE SAMUEL

GERMAN

Act 1

Scene 1

The scene is the corner of a gun-park in the British Zone of Germany, in February 1954. Centre stage is a small guard hut, very bare indeed, with four small hospital beds, a table and a chair. No pillows, no blankets, nothing to cover the floor-boards. A bit of mill-board hangs on the wall, with guard-duties etc. Outside, to the left of the hut, is a small acting area where the guard halts, and is inspected etc. It is the end of a road, which leads round behind the hut back to the barracks. There is barbed wire behind the hut, and down one side of the stage, and there is a barbed wire gate into the gun-park.

Downstage of the hut, as far away as possible, the front of a Bofors gun emerges from the wings. On the other side, against the barbed wire, is a pile of jerry-cans, and a few small boxes.

It is six o'clock on a very cold evening. Inside the hut, a German in a kind of sub-uniform — dark green, with a forage cap, but no badges — is finishing off painting the window- ledge. He is mumbling and whistling a 1954 German popsong. He finishes the job meticulously, and admires it.

At the moment, a squad of six can be heard off, marching; hearing them, he looks at his watch and unhurriedly puts away his materials.

LANCE-BOMBARDIER EVANS' VOICE: **(offstage)** 'Eft-'igh, 'eft-'igh, 'eft-'igh. **(This does not sound very military nor very convincing.)** Keep in step, there, can't you?

A squad of six Gunners comes on behind the hut. On the command 'Left wheel' from the Lance-Bombardier, they wheel in to the side of the hut, where the door is. They stop in the light of a naked bulb above the door.

EVANS: Guard: halt! Right turn! Order arms! Stanna' – ease! Staneasy –

They are all dressed in berets with Royal Artillery badges, greatcoats, full webbing-packs, belts, etc. on the outside, and carry rifles – the Old Lea-Enfield type. They are not particularly smart, nor particularly shambolic. The Lance-Bombardier has one stripe on each arm, and does not carry webbing or a rifle. He is obviously nervous, and very young. He faces the guard. They are:

GUNNER SHONE: A twenty-year-old Lancashire man, almost at the end of his National Service. He is practical and stupid, but friendly.

GUNNER FLYNN: A thirty-two-year-old hard man; a bitter ex-Irish Protestant, with no patience for anything or anybody, except possibly EVANS, with whom he is friendly. It is possible that he studied philosophy at a university, but more likely that he acquired a few ideas which simply bolstered up his already-developed feelings from extensive private study. He is thin-lipped and has a melodious voice.

GUNNER CRAWLEY: At twenty-three he is finishing off a five-year engagement. A large, thick-set, solid Yorkshireman with an aggressively loud voice, and an uncompromising manner. He plays the mouth-organ, very badly, but with enthusiasm.

GUNNER ROWE: A small, ineffective, weak, well-spoken Devon or Somerset man, who tries not to exist. He only gets angry — uncontrollably angry — when woken up. He keeps a pet rabbit in the coke-cellar, and will go into a shoe-shop when his National Service is over.

GUNNER FEATHERSTONE: A rough Cockney, a regular soldier of twenty-five, and a large poxy man. He has obviously got a record, in the Army and out of it, but is quite restrained in the company of his mate, who is

GUNNER O'ROURKE: Age twenty-nine. Tall, wild and desperate. An Irish bandit with a terrifying death-wish, a desperado whose humour, viciousness, drunkenness and ultimate despair come from deep within. To say he is bitter is to underestimate his scorn for himself and all life. He is uncontrollable, manic.

LANCE-BOMBARDIER EVANS is a nice boy, trying hard to be liked, and not really succeeding: he lacks a basic level of humanity. He is a Grammar School boy from the suburbs of Manchester, who has won a scholarship in mathematics to Cambridge. This is his first week as an N.C.O. and he is very unhappy about it but manages a kind of nervous sense of humour about his situation. He is eighteen and a half.

EVANS: **(to Guard)** Erm – you all heard the, er-orders for this guard. Two men on duty: one man patrols the perimeter-wire, the other man guards the gun-park itself – make sure nobody mucks about with the trucks petrol tanks, spare tyres, tool kits and so on, and keep an eye on the Bofors guns – make sure nobody interferes with them.

O'ROURKE: **(coming to attention loudly)** Question – sah!

EVANS: **(sighs.)**

O'ROURKE: Is it tonight we were expecting the Russians to attack, would you say?

EVANS: Look, O'Rourke, I know this is my first guard as guard-commander, and I know you have all been out here in Germany several months or even years longer than me, but I'd better tell you that I will not be mucked about, all right? Stand at ease, O'Rourke.

O'ROURKE: Permission to speak again – sah!

EVANS: Yes, what is it?

O'ROURKE: Now why would you say we were guarding the Bofors, Lance-Bombardier?

EVANS: Because somebody might need them later on, when the time comes.

CRAWLEY: **(coming to attention lazily)** Bombardier?

EVANS: Yes.

CRAWLEY: It's cold.

EVANS: Right, details. Gunner Flynn, Gunner Shone.

FLYNN and SHONE: **(coming to attention)** Sah!

EVANS: First detail. You will be on watch from six to eight and twelve to two: understood?

FLYNN and SHONE: Sah!

They stand at ease.

EVANS: Gunner Crawley, Gunner Rowe. **(They come to attention, say 'Sah' vaguely.)** Second detail, eight to ten, two to four, stand at ease, Gunner Featherstone, Gunner O'Rourke – **(FEATHERSTONE and O'ROURKE – they stamp their feet violently and yell)** Sah!

EVANS: **(pause: continues)** You will be on guard from ten to midnight and four in the morning until six in the morning. Understood?

FEATHERSTONE and O'ROURKE: **(yelling)** Yessah!

EVANS: Right. Supper will arrive at seven-thirty, first detail will eat after change-over. We'll keep it warm. Keep your eyes open for Sergeant Walker, Orderly Sergeant, and/or Mr Pickering, Orderly Officer. You can expect them to visit at any time, and they will definitely turn out the guard once during the night. We are supposed to be in a constant state of readiness, and that means turn out in ten seconds. OK? Right. First detail – detail – shun! Slope arms! Left-turn! To your posts – quick march! – Eft, igh, – eft, igh – eft, igh. **(FLYNN and SHONE march offstage.)** Remainder – remainder, shun! Slope arms! Fall-out!

They do so: sharp left turn, three paces quick march and then shambles. O'ROURKE however ignores this, and by the time they have finished he is in the hut. He sniffs loudly, and gazes at the GERMAN, who is almost ready to go.

O'ROURKE: This place stinks of paint.

OTHERS: Oh, no, stroll on, bloody hell, etc.

O'ROURKE: And who made it stink of paint? Behold the culprit.

FEATHERSTONE: It's a native.

O'ROURKE: Look at the state of him. He's dripped all over himself. **(to GERMAN)** Ach, guten Abend, mein Kraut.

The GERMAN looks rather sour, and turns away to finish packing his bag, distrustfully. EVANS comes to the door.

EVANS: Leave him alone, for God's sake, O'Rourke. What's he done to you?

O'ROURKE: Do you think he's a hero of the Resistance.

GERMAN: Please?

EVANS: Let him past, O'Rourke.

O'ROURKE: **(charming)** Of course,

EVANS: **(to GERMAN)** For cleaning the place up, we would like to say thank you.

GERMAN: **(not understanding)** Bitte?

EVANS: Er – danke.

GERMAN: Danke?

EVANS: Ja – er – danke.

GERMAN: Oh – bitte. Bitte.

EVANS: Bitte?

GERMAN: Ja – bitteschon.

EVANS: Oh – dankeschon.

GERMAN: Please?

O'ROURKE taps the GERMAN on the shoulder. When he turns, O'ROURKE screams.

O'ROURKE: **(to GERMAN)** Heil Hitler.

O'ROURKE salutes. The astounded GERMAN makes to reply and stops.

EVANS: O'Rourke!

O'ROURKE: **(snarls)** Ha-ha-ha.

EVANS: O'Rourke!

O'ROURKE: Ah rot off, Fritz.

The GERMAN goes.

EVANS: Why couldn't you leave the poor bastard alone? What's he done to you?

O'ROURKE: **(shouting after GERMAN)** You know what German house painters grow up into, don't you, Fritz?

GERMAN: **(turns defiantly, but not quite sure what he is saying)** Baw-lawks.

O'ROURKE: Oh, did you hear what he said? **(Laughing, pleased with the GERMAN)** Cunning little bugger – fancy him saying that to me. **(Meanwhile, the others have laid themselves flat out on the beds, and lit up cigarettes.)** Here, why have I got the bed by the door? I'll get earache. Listen, is your name Rowe?

ROWE: Yes, what of it?

O'ROURKE: Well, Rowe yourself over to the other pit, we're doing a swap.

ROWE: But I got here first.

O'ROURKE: That may well be, but what you're not taking into account is that I am bigger, and stronger, than you are, and a damn sight more desperate. So shift.

They stare each other out. EVANS looks on, powerless. Eventually ROWE breaks.

ROWE: **(shrugging)** Ah, sod it.

O'ROURKE: **(blessing him)** In nomine patris et filii – Go with God, my child, and go in gladness, for the first shall be the last, and the last shall be the first. And blessed are the pure of heart. **(Stretches out.)** Aah. It's a man's life in the Regular Army, push us a fag, Crawley. **(CRAWLEY passes him a packet, from which he takes one, and then throws the packet back. He stretches out an imperial arm for a light, and CRAWLEY passes him his cigarette, which he uses and passes back. He exhales with a sigh. Then he chuckles quietly and happily to himself.)** Bawlawks. Fancy that now. **(Imitates the GERMAN.)** Baw-lawks, Ha.

He subsides, Silence. Establish the atmosphere of the place, the fatigue, the waiting, the warmth. EVANS sits, his head in his hands, gazing into space. The others lie on the beds, smoking, dreaming. CRAWLEY is sitting up a bit, concentrating.

CRAWLEY: **(slowly)** Who works out who does what night?

Pause.

FEATHERSTONE: Eh?

CRAWLEY: What rotten pox-etten bombardier works out who does what guard when? **(Pause. They ignore him.)** What I mean is, what bombardier sitting on what potty puts me on guard every pay-night?

O'ROURKE: It's just your horrible luck, soldier.

FEATHERSTONE: 'Ere, are you a Catholic, O'Rourke?

O'ROURKE: Balls.

FEATHERSTONE: I thought you was. How old are you?

CRAWLEY: **(persisting)** What pissy-knickered bombardier sits down every Friday in the Regimental Sergeant Major's bungalow, spits the boot polish out of his mouth from licking the R.S.M.'s boots, and says to himself: 'Right, Gunner Crawley 307, no pay night piss-up for you, gunner, no revels with your muckers in the NAAFI, no two sausage, egg and chips for you, mate, no wunderbar wunderbeer downtown in the Y.M., no – nothing like that, soldier – you're on rotten guard.' Who is it says that, then?

O'ROURKE: I'm three hundred and two.

CRAWLEY: **(throwing something at ROWE)** Who is it says that? Have you all gone deaf?

ROWE: I don't know. I sometimes wonder if the Almighty might not have a finger in it.

FEATHERSTONE: **(mimicking)** Oh, 'e wondahs if the Ormaghtey mate not 'ev a fingah up it.

CRAWLEY: **(to ROWE, scornfully)** What do you mean by that?

ROWE: Do you know something, Featherstone?

FEATHERSTONE: No, Rowe, I don't know. What was you going to impart?

ROWE: **(turning away)** Ah . . .

FEATHERSTONE: What? Go on, say it, brother Rowe, let's hear it.

ROWE: **(to the wall)** You've got B. O.

FEATHERSTONE: Eh?

ROWE: **(whipping round and whispering loudly right into his face)** Bee Oh . . .

FEATHERSTONE: **(not batting an eyelid)** Do you find it offensive then? **(They look at each other, then with a calculated, non-emotional response, FEATHERSTONE takes him with one hand by the back of the neck.)** Look, Sonny, you're going the right way to get your little head knocked off. **(He gets more vicious, pulls his head very close to him, and forces his mouth open by squeezing his cheeks together with thumb and finger.)** Come a bit closer, Gunner Rowe. Let Uncle Freddie smell your breath. Open wide. **(He examines his mouth, then gets suddenly quite serious.)** Hey, Your gums are rotting. Bloody hell he's got siphylitic teeth. Look at that. Look, it's true isn't it? Here – how do you manage to catch pox there then – you dirty bastard.

CRAWLEY goes over and looks.

CRAWLEY: **(professionally)** Trench-mouth.

FEATHERSTONE: Since when has he been in a trench? Bombardier! Bombardier! Eh Bom, I object. **(He pushes ROWE away who rubs his face. He does not care in the slightest about having trench-mouth.)** It's unhygenic.

I've got my rights, and I object to being obliged to kip, all night, in a little hut with an infected sex-maniac. So if it's all right by you, Bom, can I go home? Eh? **(They look at EVANS, who is sitting, with his elbows on the table, his head in his hands, and his fingers plugged in his ears, gazing, lost, into space.)** Hey, look at him. Is it past your bed-time, little man? Have you had a busy day? Ah it must be hard.

As they realise he's not with them, and can't hear a word, they sit up and get interested.

CRAWLEY: **(having a go)** Oh bombardier oh bombardier,

They say you can't hold half a beer.

They laugh. He takes no notice.

ROWE: Hey, somebody told me he's all lined up to be an officer.

CRAWLEY: What him?

ROWE: Mm, He failed his wasp or something, but they're sending him back to Blighty, to try it again.

CRAWLEY: What's a wasp?

ROWE: To be an officer.

FEATHERSTONE: Stroll on. Did you hear that, Rourkey?

O'ROURKE: I hear you soldier. He'll make a beautiful subaltern. Lovely bone-structure. Fine arse on him.

CRAWLEY: Eh, is it true that all the Second Lieutenants have to bend over for the C.O.?

O'ROURKE: True? By Jesus, they'd be court-martialled and cashiered and reduced to the ranks at the double if they didn't. **(To EVANS)** Isn't that so, my beauty? Look at him blush. I swear he can hear us. **(Laughs, making kissing noises)** Give us a kiss.

CRAWLEY: **(sings again)** Oh bombardier oh bombardier

They say you're looking mighty queer.

FEATHERSTONE: Do you think he's Kosher?

O'ROURKE: Not him, devil a bit of it. A fancy-boy may be, but he's too pig-ignorant for a Jew. Aren't you Terry Evans?

CRAWLEY: Bloody hell, he's a good way off into dreamland all the same.

FEATHERSTONE: I tell you what, let's drop the bastard in it. Let's all scarper.

CRAWLEY: Let's all get pissed.

O'ROURKE: Let's do for him, the kind-hearted gobshite.

CRAWLEY: We could all creep off to the NAAFI one by one, until when the Orderly Officer came to turn out the guard, the whole bloody lot was away with the mixer.

ROWE: Ah now, that's a bit uncalled for. He means well, I think. Besides he might drop us in it first, you never can tell.

O'ROURKE laughs.

FEATHERSTONE: Sh! He's coming round.

EVANS shakes his head, and gazes round.

EVANS: How goes the enemy?

FEATHERSTONE: Mm?

CRAWLEY: The enemy?

O'ROURKE: The Russians is it?

EVANS: Sorry, **(yawns)** I meant the time.

FEATHERSTONE: Haven't you got a watch then, Lance Bombardier?

EVANS: Me? Oh yes, so I have: Army issue, guard commanders for the use of. **(Pulls one out of his pocket.)** Oh dear. Hours to supper-time.

He gets up, apparently very relaxed, goes out and round the back of the hut, where there is a latrine.

CRAWLEY: Ah, he's no more than a lad, bless his heart. He's no more than a boy.

Pause.

FEATHERSTONE: Maybe it's up to us to turn him into a soldier.

Pause.

O'ROURKE: You're an evil man, Featherstone, an evil minded man.

He sings:
Oh I wasn't drunk and I wasn't blind
When I left my two fine legs behind:
For a cannon-ball on the fifth of May
Took my two fine legs from the knees away.
With a toori-ah, toori-addy-ah
Toori-oori-oori-ah.

At the end of O'ROURKE's song, CRAWLEY plunges with feeling into a romantic ballad on the mouth-organ. The others lie back, sleep, smoke, scratch themselves etc. EVANS appears from the back of the hut, but doesn't go in. He walks to the downstage corner of the hut and looks out

over the gun-park, huddled up, his hands in his pocket, to keep himself from freezing.

EVANS: Rot this for a life. **(Smiles. Goes into slight routine)**: I say, I say, I say – it was so cold – it was so cold, do you know, – no, it's true. It was so cold I saw a dog frozen to a tree. Fresh frozen pees. **(Laughter. Then sees something on the horizon.)** Look at that. The size of that moon is just not natural. It's not natural.

As he stares in wonder at the moon, FLYNN enters stamping his feet and blowing quietly on his hands on the other side of the stage. EVANS and FLYNN are friends, and share a barrack-room, but they are very different types, and there's a wariness of each other as well as warmth.

EVANS: Bill!

FLYNN: Yes, who's that?

EVANS: Me, Terry.

FLYNN: Oh, hello. Taking the air?

EVANS: **(crossing down to him)** Yes. That hut stinks of bodies.

FLYNN: Already? You wait till six in the morning.

Pause.

EVANS: Did you notice the moon? Is it natural to have such an enormous moon?

FLYNN: **(not looking)** Ah now it must be them H. Bombs. Who's that playing the mouth organ? He ought to learn not to blow when he's supposed to be sucking.

EVANS: **(still thinking of the moon)** Mm – **(Pause.)** Do you think it could be a harvest-size moon, Bill?

FLYNN: In February? No, I believe it's what they call a Hunter's Moon: though I don't suppose anybody hunts by it. Except foxes, of course.

Pause.

EVANS: Do you want to know something, Bill?

FLYNN: Mm? What's that?

EVANS: I've only got tonight to push.

FLYNN: What does that mean?

EVANS: I've only got to get through tonight, Bill, and I'm off: I'm going back home tomorrow for an Officer Selection Board. I just found out. Four o'clock train. Night-boat from the Hook. Harwich Sunday morning. Woolwich Sunday afternoon. Manchester Sunday night. How about that?

FLYNN: **(pleased)** You crafty bugger. Fancy not letting on.

EVANS: I swear to you I just found out, but don't tell the others, Bill —

FLYNN: Well well, what about that: I can't pretend I'm not jealous. In fact I'm green with envy, sod you. But that's great. Really great.

EVANS: I'm glad you're pleased.

FLYNN: Well what did you expect?

EVANS: I don't know. I thought — well — privileges, getting on: they're not popular.

FLYNN: **(laughing)** Ha, you're going to be a successful man, Terry, and there's no point in fighting it; and you want it, don't you?

EVANS: If it comes, it comes, if it doesn't, sod it. My dad sells paraffin in Wythenshawe. What do I want to be an officer for?

FLYNN: Of course.

EVANS: I suppose you don't?

FLYNN: What? I don't what?

EVANS: Want to get on.

FLYNN: Ah well, not really. No, I don't think I do.

Pause. EVANS is worried by this.

EVANS: Er — is it true Bill that you wouldn't take a stripe?

FLYNN: If I wouldn't take a pip, I wouldn't take a stripe now would I?

EVANS: Do you mean you —

FLYNN: I have no desire for improvement. Besides, you've never been in an Officers' Mess, have you?

EVANS: Er — no, I don't suppose I have.

FLYNN: Well I had the misfortune to be brought up in one to the age of ten. A strict sort of infancy it was.

EVANS: Really?

FLYNN: I've never been into an Officers' Mess, since. Nor shall I. I prefer animals. **(Pause.)** Besides, my father was shot.

EVANS: I'm sorry. I didn't know. **(Pause.)** I wondered why you hadn't got on.

FLYNN: **(laughs a little too loudly)** Dear old Lance Bombardier, you're a terribly nice bloke, but you must admit you're a bit of a simpleton —

EVANS: Am I?

FLYNN: Do you suppose everybody wants to get on?

EVANS: Well — in a way.

FLYNN: **(laughs again)** That's the stuff that built the Empire. Well, tell me, why isn't O'Rourke a sergeant and Featherstone a colonel? Because they're too stupid, do you think?

EVANS: I don't know. But somebody has got to be an officer, and carry the can.

FLYNN: Don't let it be me, that's all I ask. Never be on the side of the judges, Terry – my motto for the day.

EVANS: No. I suppose not.

FLYNN: I despise people who are taken in: by pips and stripes and wigs and chains.

EVANS: Does that include me Bill?

A long silence. They look at each other. Then Flynn breaks it, smiles, pats EVANS on the shoulder affectionately and says

FLYNN: Good luck with it, Terry. I mean that.

FLYNN moves off leaving EVANS alone. Pause. He gets up. He goes over and into the hut. He opens the door, and stands half inside looking at the moon. The others look up aggressively.

CHORUS: Shut the bloody door!

He comes in.

O'ROURKE: Anything to report, sir? Are the Chinese advancing?

EVANS: Haven't you heard? The Chinese advance sideways.

O'ROURKE: Ohoho, show us your legs.

EVANS: That'll do, O'Rourke. Don't get carried away.

O'ROURKE: I won't, Bom, I promise I won't. Besides, the night is young.

The phone rings. EVANS answers it. The others listen. He uses his best voice.

EVANS: Gun-park guard room . . . Bombardier Evans speaking sir . . . very good sir, I'll see to that sir . . . **(laughs)** well yes I was hoping to sir . . . **(beams, pleased)** Thank you very much sir . . . Goodnight to you sir.

He puts the phone down, but the aura, the fixed smile of conversation with a superior remains momentarily. The others gaze upon it, nudge each other, and wink.

O'ROURKE: Now who was that, Bom. It sounded dreadfully important to me.

EVANS: If the temperature drops below ten degrees Fahrenheit, we've got to wake up the drivers. They'll have to empty the radiators in case the Anti-freeze freezes.

O'ROURKE: He sounded most charming.

EVANS: **(ignores this)** Don't forget then. There's a thermometer on the radiator of the fifteen hundredweight under the light – check it every hour or so.

25

O'ROURKE: **(saluting)** Yes Bom.

EVANS begins to put his papers in order.

FEATHERSTONE: Er, Terry –

EVANS: Yes? I – I suppose you'd better call me Bombardier, do you mind?

FEATHERSTONE: No, I don't mind. I thought you might mind, really. It's not what you call matey, having all your mates call you Bombardier. Still – if that's the way you want it, Terry, Amen, so be it.

EVANS: It's not so much that I want to be called Bombardier, it's just – well, I think it might be better – do you see what I mean?

FEATHERSTONE: Yes. So we know where we stand sort of thing.

O'ROURKE: **(looking at the ceiling)** That's right, so we all know our place: some run with the foxes, some hunt with the hounds.

EVANS: Well, it's not so much that even –

O'ROURKE: A – a. Can't run with both now, Bombardier, can we?

EVANS: Well no, but –

O'ROURKE: **(sits up)** Tell me though, do you feel yourself, – at heart, you know – do you feel yourself to be a fox man or a hound man? That interests me that.

EVANS: **(quietly)** I'm against Blood Sports, on the whole.

O'ROURKE: **(cackles)** Is that so? By God you're the clever bastard at getting out of things, I'll hand you that. Wouldn't you say that now. Featherstone my old butty?

FEATHERSTONE: Definitely. **(Not knowing what the question was.)**

O'ROURKE: Ignorant Englishman.

FEATHERSTONE: What I would like to say is: does the bombardier realise that tonight is pay-night?

EVANS: Er – yes, he does.

FEATHERSTONE: That being the case, I ask myself, would the bombardier grant his kind permission to me and my friend O'Rourke here, to swan off into the NAAFI and buy ourselves our little fag ration, before they all go?

CRAWLEY: Here, – leave off, do – you're not on guard till ten o'clock, I'm on at bloody eight. By the time I come off at ten, the NAAFI'll be closed.

FEATHERSTONE: Oh no it bloody won't mate.

CRAWLEY: **(loud)** Of course it bloody will, don't be stupid, ten o'clock.

FEATHERSTONE: Look, who asked first?

O'ROURKE: First come, first served, Crawley me old mate.

CRAWLEY: **(louder)** Oh do leave off, can't you? – Rowe, here, are you just going to lie there and let them two rotten baskets get away with it? Well are you?

ROWE has his face to the wall, lying on his bed.

FEATHERSTONE: **(quietly)** Here, he's having a crafty J. Arthur,

CRAWLEY: **(impressed)** The sneaky hypocrite. **(To ROWE)**: Here, you'll grow hairs on the palm of your hands if you do that, lad.

Suddenly ROWE does a violent snort, and turns over. He is fast asleep.

O'ROURKE: Aw now isn't that lovely? He's fast asleep. Will you look at the little secret smile he has on him. Tell us, Gunner Rowe, what's your inner man so pleased at?

FEATHERSTONE: Here, I'll tell you why he's laughing, here –

He whispers a few words to O'ROURKE, who is not amused and pushes him away sharply.

O'ROURKE: You're a disgusting obscene pig, Featherstone, likewise all Cockneys. I never knew one with a pennyworth of taste. You've a vile tongue and a vile mind, and whereas I don't give a silent fart for indecent expressions, the dwelling on sperm that goes on in your mind is repellent to say the least. Tell me, Gunner Featherstone, do you Cockneys have problems?

FEATHERSTONE: I'd do you for that, O'Rourke, if you wasn't a lunatic . . .

O'ROURKE: Ha ha . . .

FEATHERSTONE: Do you know what he done the other night? He put his hand in the stove in the front guard-room, and pulled out a red-hot lump of coke. Didn't you? And he held it there till it burnt a great big hole in his hand. Go on, show the people. **(O'ROURKE looks at it himself, but will not show the others.)** I told you, you're a lunatic. **(To others)** He's more to be pitied, really.

EVANS: What did you do that for?

O'ROURKE: **(harshly)** Are you talking to me, Bombardier?

EVANS: Er, yes – I wondered what made you do it, that's all.

O'ROURKE: I'm glad you find me of interest, Bombardier.

EVANS: I'm sorry. I didn't mean to sound patronising. I really would like to know.

O'ROURKE: **(spitefully)** You would, would you – well I'll tell you. It was the company. I couldn't stand the company I was in. Do you follow me? Weaklings and hypocrites – bed-wetters one and all.

CRAWLEY: Did you go sick?

O'ROURKE: Of course not. It was a gesture, no more.

Awkward pause.

FEATHERSTONE: Yes, well. Who makes the gesture of going for the fags then? **(To CRAWLEY)** You, or us?

EVANS: Can't one of you get them for everybody?

CRAWLEY: No, Bom, we can't, because of the chitties. No man gets more than two hundred and forty cheap fags per week, – it's scandalous. I know a bloke who saved up chitties for seven thousand cheap fags, for when he went home. He would have made a fortune in Woolwich. Then out comes this new regulation in the NAAFI, and where is he? The bottom's fallen out of the market. He has to sell them off at twopence for a twenty chitty to blokes who smoke more than two hundred and forty fags a week. Well, that's no life, is it?

FEATHERSTONE: Still, if he sells seven thousand at twopence for twenty, he makes a bob or two, you know.

CRAWLEY: How much would you say he'd get, all together?

FEATHERSTONE: I'm glad you asked me that, because I can tell you.

CRAWLEY: Get away, Go on then, how much?

FEATHERSTONE: Well he'd get tenpence for a hundred, that's eight and fourpence for a thousand, isn't it, that's seven times ten bob is three pounds ten less seven eightpences that's fifty-six is four and eightpence, so he'd get three pounds five and fourpence less seven shillings is two pounds eighteen shillings and fourpence – Less Income Tax,

CRAWLEY: Bastard stroll on. That's not much, is it?

FEATHERSTONE: He couldn't live on it, not at two pounds eighteen and fourpence for two years' work. Do you know what that works out at per week?

CRAWLEY: Don't bother, mastermind, we can guess.

FEATHERSTONE: Well, it's . . .

O'ROURKE: Forget it, can't you? Don't go showing off your affliction to the nice bombardier. **(Gets up.)** Now then, who's for the canteen? I think we've had enough of this bloody shed.

EVANS: Have you all got to go?

FEATHERSTONE: Well, it's only fair, Bom, I mean, why should we be penalised just because we're on guard-duty? It should be the other way around, shouldn't it? I mean, if we have to leave it till tomorrow they'll have run out, and then we won't get our fags till Monday. Well, that's hardly justice, is it?

EVANS: I suppose it's not. But Crawley and Rowe had better go first. You can't all go at once, that's for certain, and I'm not sure that any of you should go when you're on guard –

CRAWLEY: Aw eh, Bombardier . . .

EVANS: So it's Rowe and Crawley now, and Featherstone and O'Rourke, after supper. And no mucking about. Is that clear?

ALL: Yes, yes, absolutely, depend on us, etc.

O'ROURKE is standing, ready to go, but decides against having a showdown so soon.

O'ROURKE: You can rely on us, Bombardier. No mucking about.

He gives a large, obvious wink at FEATHERSTONE, and crosses back to his bed with an air of defiance. EVANS notices, but pretends not to.

EVANS: Right, well – **(looks at watch)** – I suppose the first two had better push off now, before the meal gets here: there's not so long.

CRAWLEY: Will I wake Rowe, Bom?

EVANS: Er, yes, give him a shake.

CRAWLEY lifts the top of ROWE's bed and drops it. ROWE is deeply asleep and childishly annoyed. He sits up, furious.

ROWE: Who did that?

CRAWLEY: I did. Bombardier's orders.

ROWE: Well rot him.

He goes back to sleep. CRAWLEY lifts the head and drops it again.

ROWE: Rot off

CRAWLEY does it again, cheerfully.

CRAWLEY: Rowe. Oh wake up you daft get, come on.

ROWE bellows, lying.

ROWE: Why can't you leave me in peace?

CRAWLEY: Because the bombardier said we were both to go to the NAAFI, to pick up our fags.

ROWE: Jesus Christ!

CRAWLEY: Well come on.

ROWE: I don't bloody smoke, that's all.

He goes back to sleep. CRAWLEY shrugs.

CRAWLEY: Right then, I'll go on my own. Can I fetch anything for you Bom? A beer or something?

EVANS: No thanks, Crawley. Not in the guard-room. But thanks for the thought.

CRAWLEY: Oh that's all right, Bombardier. I just thought that as you was a notorious drinking man, you might begin to get desperate for a pint before the night's out. Never mind. You can always take snuff.

He goes, loudly whistling away.

FEATHERSTONE: Stupid swede he is. **(Lies back comfortably. Mimics.)** Would you like a beer Bombardier? That's Lancashire wit, that is!

O'ROURKE: **(lying on his back)** Did I ever tell you, Featherstone, about the time I was a sergeant in the Irish Dragoons?

FEATHERSTONE: **(imitating the GERMAN)** Baw-lawks.

O'ROURKE: No, it's true, quite true. I remember it well. **(Sings)**

There was a troop of Irish Dragoons
Came riding down to Fivey – oh –

Where the hell did I put my matches?

EVANS: Were you really a sergeant once, O'Rourke?

O'ROURKE: Don't question me about my past, Bombardier. I prefer to let it recede into the mists of sweet forgetfulness.

There is a silence. The wind whistles. The lights dim imperceptibly. FEATHERSTONE sits up, lights O'ROURKE's fag. Then he makes spooky music noises, quietly.

FEATHERSTONE: Isn't that spooky? Here, shall I tell you this film I seen?

EVANS: What was it called?

FEATHERSTONE: I don't know. It was all about this man who seen the devil: in a graveyard.

EVANS: **(laughs)** In a graveyard?

O'ROURKE: I know a fellow saw the devil: In a field. And this was no film.

EVANS: Oh come on, now, O'Rourke – don't give us the blarney.

O'ROURKE: You may not believe it, Bombardier, but this feller was a daily Communicant, a total abstainer and a pioneer of twelve years standing, and I do.

FEATHERSTONE: Where was this then, Danny?

O'ROURKE: It was in Ireland. In Sligo. In a field. In daylight.

FEATHERSTONE: Get away.

O'ROURKE: He said he was a little fellow, you know – not so much of a dwarf – more of a manikin kind of a thing. Perfect in every way. Absolutely perfect. Except for a hump on his back. A little hump.

EVANS: Ah now, you got that from a song, the hump on his back.

O'ROURKE: Not at all, it's a well-known fact.

FEATHERSTONE: Anyway. What was he doing?

O'ROURKE: The devil? Well now, I don't want to shock you, but he was interfering with the livestock.

FEATHERSTONE: Dirty devil.

O'ROURKE: Not in the way that immediately springs to your sperm-ridden imagination, Featherstone, but in a most peculiar fashion. You see, this cow had just had a calf, and you know after they've calved, they give off this terrible dense yellow milk, like Nestle's a bit?

EVANS: Do they really?

O'ROURKE: It's well seen you're a town boy. Anyway they do. It's disgusting stuff – they feed it to old men for rheumatism, who instantly die. However this, this yellow stuff, is, it appears, the devil's own favourite tipple, for my friend the pioneer swears to God that he seen him, on hands and knees, sucking the titties of a post-natal Guernsey, – and keeping the calf at bay with his spiky tail. And he said – and it's true, – that after he'd sucked them, they withered away.

Pause.

EVANS: **(laughs)** O'Rourke, you're a fine story-teller.

O'ROURKE suddenly jumps up and slams his hand on the table under EVANS' nose. He is wildly angry.

O'ROURKE: You didn't believe that of course, my twee little bombardier?

EVANS: I – well, you didn't expect – Oh come on, O'Rourke, I thought you were joking. Or your friend was.

O'ROURKE: Pioneers don't joke: and if you don't believe him I can tell you that the wrinkled teats I saw myself, with my own eyes. Perhaps you'll believe that.

EVANS: Well yes, of course.

O'ROURKE: Aha, You don't doubt me, do you?

EVANS: No no, of course not,

O'ROURKE: Good. Because I'm telling the truth tonight. I don't know why. **(He goes back to his bed, slightly more relaxed.)** Always tell the truth, son, my father used to say to me. Never lie, son, it'll only cause trouble. And do you know what that lying bastard told me, on the day he died? He told me that he had killed his own brother, at the age of eight, by holding his head under water until he was drowned. And he never let on to a soul.

FEATHERSTONE: Your old man told you that?

O'ROURKE: He did so. Four hours before he died. And he obliged me, likewise, to keep it a secret until – ah well, the old bugger won't be worrying now, wherever he is, will he? **(Pause.)** Do you doubt me, Bombardier?

EVANS: Er – No, I don't.

FEATHERSTONE: Until when Danny?

O'ROURKE: Oh, you know – the day I die or something.

EVANS: Really

O'ROURKE, on hearing this, gives a manic laugh, half derisive and half hysterical, and then stops, winks at FEATHERSTONE, sits on his bed, and hums loudly and violently, the air of the 'Troop of Irish Dragoons', as the lights dim to Blackout.

Scene 2

Fade up. The same, an hour later. EVANS is sleeping in the chair, his head on the table. The others, except O'ROURKE, sleep on the beds. O'ROURKE is sitting up straight, staring into space. O'ROURKE finishes the song. A noise off-stage, and SAMUEL, a cook-private, approaches, carrying food-cans and whistling. He kicks at the door, and O'ROURKE goes and opens it with a flourish. The others, except ROWE, wake up dozily, and pay attention. O'ROURKE's mood changes violently.

O'ROURKE: Ah the picnic has arrived at last. What is it tonight, Samuel?

SAMUEL: Cauliflower cheese.

O'ROURKE: I can't wait.

SAMUEL: Hope it chokes you.

EVANS: Is Sergeant Walker creeping around, did you notice?

SAMUEL: I don't know, do I? Here, sign that.

EVANS signs a chitty. SAMUEL takes it and goes.

O'ROURKE: **(shouting down ROWE's ear)** Nosebag-time, Gunner Rowe!

He picks up ROWE's bed and drops it. There is a pause then ROWE sits up and looks at O'ROURKE.

ROWE: Why don't you go interfere with your mother, Irishman?

O'ROURKE walks quietly over to him, hits him very hard in the stomach, which doubles him up on the bed, and looks at him.

O'ROURKE: Don't provoke me, Rowe. **(He turns away and sits on the end of a**

bed. FEATHERSTONE is dishing out the food on the floor.) Get me some of the swill, Featherstone. **(FEATHERSTONE makes up a meal and hands it up to him. ROWE is making retching noises behind him. He takes the meal, and turns to ROWE.)** How are we expected to eat with that noise going on? Control yourself, can't you? **(He sits looking at the meal in disgust, and listening to ROWE. Then he stands, looks at ROWE, goes to the door and slings his food out into the fire-bucket outside. He comes back in and sits on the bed again. The silence is resumed. Then)**: Well, Bombardier; why don't you put me on a charge?

EVANS: **(strongly)** That was pretty bloody stupid, O'Rourke, and unnecessary. I don't care what you do with your cauliflower cheese, but there was no justification for hitting Rowe like that, none whatever.

O'ROURKE: Well why don't you put me on a charge?

EVANS: I know he insulted you, and that's bad, but –

O'ROURKE: **(harsh)** I hit him for no reason.

EVANS: Don't speak to me like that, O'Rourke, there is no point in inviting disaster. All I am saying is that you were stupid and rash to act in that way, and –

O'ROURKE: Bombardier I've had quite enough of your innermost thoughts, and I'm here to tell you you're no bloody Einstein – will you answer me straight: do I get on a charge or don't I?

EVANS: No, I see no point in that –

O'ROURKE: Thank you. I'll say three Hail Marys, and pray God for forgiveness. **(Takes plate off the floor, hands it to ROWE.)** Here, Rowe, eat up your din-dins. Next time I'll kill you. **(ROWE takes the plate, and avoiding O'ROURKE's eye, he begins to eat. O'ROURKE moves into his own bed, stretches out, takes a cigarette out of his pocket, lights it and throws the pack away.)** I hope Crawley's back quick. This is my last. **(A moody silence while the others eat, and O'ROURKE smokes his cigarette. ROWE sniffs several times.)** Stop sniffing Rowe, I've said my three Hail Marys. **(The others look up, then carry on eating. O'ROURKE is tense, his body is rigid and his foot is tapping against the end of the bed. He sings, harshly.)**

> Oh then Ted me boy, the widow cried,
> Yer two fine legs were ye mammy's pride.
> Them stumps of a tree wouldn't do at all,
> Why didn't you run from the big cannon ball?
>
> With a toori-ah, toori-addy-ah,
> Toori, oori, oori-.ah.

(More tension, more tapping on the bed. He rolls over and says to FEATHERSTONE, who is by now lying on the next bed.) I've got a great idea, Alexander. I think I'm going to get pissed and jump off the water-tower.

FEATHERSTONE: Ah shut up, Danny, you're giving me the curse.

O'ROURKE: Do you think I'm joking? I am not so.

EVANS: O'Rourke

O'ROURKE: Hey-ho, another portion of confessional advice. Yes, sonny, what is it you want?

EVANS: I want to tell you that you, for one, are not getting pissed tonight.

O'ROURKE: **(stands, violent movement)** Where's Crawley? He's on guard in ten minutes, where is he?

FEATHERSTONE: Ah leave off, Danny —

O'ROURKE: I need some fags, I tell you, this is my last.

FEATHERSTONE: Here, have one of mine.

O'ROURKE: Not at all, I'm smoking.

FEATHERSTONE: Well what's up with you then?

O'ROURKE: I can't get on without a full packet of fags — I like the weight of them, in the pocket. Pleasant to finger.

FEATHERSTONE: I know what you like.

O'ROURKE: What? What's that?

FEATHERSTONE: Sit down and relax, Danny. You're like an old meths-drinker there. You and your craving.

O'ROURKE: **(laughs)** And how would you know? **(To EVANS)** He's suggesting that I'm an alcoholic, Bombardier, did you hear that?

EVANS: He's probably dead right.

O'ROURKE: **(laughs again, pleased)** Where the hell's Crawley?

FEATHERSTONE: Give us another song, Danny. That'll cheer you up. One of them jiggy ones.

O'ROURKE: Ah rot off!

FEATHERSTONE: No, go on. I like them jiggy ones, they're very Irish.

O'ROURKE: And how the hell would you know?

FEATHERSTONE: Well, you can tell.

O'ROURKE: Do you mean like 'Knees up Mother Brown', now that's very Irish.

FEATHERSTONE: What's got into you tonight? Needing your oats or something?

O'ROURKE: I had what you call my oats last night. I do not need them again tonight. As a matter of fact, after last night's experiences, I shall never need them again. Where the hell is Crawley? He's going to be late for the change over. Where is he?

FEATHERSTONE: Relax, can't you? He'll get here. Anyway, Flynn should be doing the worrying, not you.

O'ROURKE: Flynn? Is he that smart feller, the tight-lipped bastard? It'll do him good to wait in the cold, that's one consolation.

FEATHERSTONE: Do you know something: I think that bloke's an iron –

O'ROURKE: A what?

FEATHERSTONE: A pouf.

ROWE: What? Flynn? Of course he's not.

FEATHERSTONE: And how do you know he's not?

O'ROURKE: He's tried him.

FEATHERSTONE: I reckon he's bent: don't you Bombardier?

EVANS: I've no idea.

FEATHERSTONE: Oh, I thought he was a friend of yours.

Pause. Then.

ROWE: For your information, Featherstone, old Flynn had more carnal knowledge before he was sixteen, then you'll have in the rest of your life.

FEATHERSTONE: You're joking of course.

ROWE: As a matter of fact, I'm not.

FEATHERSTONE: Get on. How's that then?

ROWE: He had this schoolgirl, him and his mate.

FEATHERSTONE: Get away.

ROWE: He was fourteen, and she was twelve. He told me. Him and his mate used to take it in turns. Every night. Five times a night. For two years.

FEATHERSTONE: Then what happened? Why did he stop?

ROWE: She got one in the oven; she's gone down in medical history.

FEATHERSTONE: Is that true?

ROWE: Absolutely.

FEATHERSTONE: And what happened to Flynn?

ROWE: I don't know. I suppose he misses it.

FEATHERSTONE: There you are, I told you he was a pouf.

EVANS: Don't be ridiculous.

FEATHERSTONE: What do you think, Danny, isn't he a pouf.

O'ROURKE: Do you really want to know what I think?

FEATHERSTONE: What's that then?

O'ROURKE: I think the entire English are a race of frustrated sex-criminals, and the whole lot of you's perverted. As a matter of fact you make me sick.

FEATHERSTONE: Well well.

Offstage, the sounds of CRAWLEY's approach.

O'ROURKE: Here's Crawley! **(He grabs his great-coat hastily and starts pulling it on.)** Come on, Featherstone, the NAAFI awaits. England expects this night every man to do his duty. **(CRAWLEY comes in, closes the door, and heads for the stove. He has had a pint or two, but is not drunk. He gets to the fire and belches.)** Grand night, Crawley!

CRAWLEY: Brass monkey weather. I just seen one wearing a support. My advice: stay at home.

O'ROURKE: Oh but we can't do that. The Bombardier says we must guard the Bofors Gun: for who will do it, if not us?

CRAWLEY: Here are you going on second turn?

O'ROURKE: No, we are not. We are going to the NAAFI canteen. **(Winks.)** For fags.

EVANS: **(stands up to them)** Look, O'Rourke and Featherstone – you have permission to go to the NAAFI, buy your cigarette ration for the week, and then come straight back. Is that quite clear?

FEATHERSTONE: Yes, Bom.

O'ROURKE: Absolutely, Bom. **(They are at the door.)** Er – by the way, Bom, what'll you do if we don't, like, settle for fags?

EVANS: You know very well what I'd have to do, Inform Sergeant Walker. What else could I do?

O'ROURKE: You'd never charge us yourself, like? – Oh no, of course, no no, you wouldn't do that, would you? You're such a nice, gentle creature, such a – saintly man, almost. My mother would think he was a sure tip for a saint, do you know that? Saint Terence – Virgin and Martyr.

EVANS: **(standing)** O'Rourke, you really make me think I should charge you here and now.

O'ROURKE: **(looking at him levelly)** You are a fool not to. I should not be at large.

EVANS: Piss off.

O'ROURKE: A – a. That's not nice. Besides it's irresponsible.

EVANS: Make sure you are back within half an hour.

O'ROURKE: Good-night, Bombardier.

They go. The others gaze at EVANS. After a while, ROWE gently breaks the silence.

ROWE: They'll not come back, you know, Bombardier.

EVANS: Oh I think they will. They're not as bad as they let on to be.

ROWE: They're half insane. Besides, O'Rourke's well known to be almost an alcoholic. And every time he gets drunk he runs amok.

EVANS: Oh don't be like that. If you trust people, they won't muck you about. It's all these restrictions that do the harm.

CRAWLEY: Last Christmas it took four M.P.s to stop him breaking up this dance-hall. And them. And himself.

ROWE: And three months before that, out on an exercise, he climbed up a pylon, pissed as a fart, and swung hand over hand along the wire; then he dropped off, into a pond, and they had to carry him back to the dug-out. And before that, last summer –

EVANS: Thank you, Rowe. I think I get the picture. **(Looks at his watch.)** It's time to change over.

ROWE: Oh, righto Bom: we're nearly ready.

They put on their gear quickly, take their rifles, and go.

ROWE: **(at the door)** I hope it's all right, Bom.

They go. EVANS is alone. He is very worried.

Blackout.

Scene 3

Fade up. No curtain. In the hut, the main light is out, and FLYNN and SHONE are sleeping. EVANS sits at the table, gazing into space. It is 9.35, and the others are not back.

Downstage, CRAWLEY is sitting on a gun-wheel, or a box, smoking secretly, and making very quiet, nonconsequent noises on the mouth organ. ROWE comes on, whispering.

ROWE: Crawley! Psst, Crawley! **(He comes up behind him, then, louder.)** Crawley!

CRAWLEY jumps up, palms his cigarette and turns, expecting the Orderly Officer.

CRAWLEY: Rowe! You rotten basket.

ROWE: What's up?

CRAWLEY: I very nearly swallowed my mouth organ.

ROWE: Sorry.

CRAWLEY: So you should be. You could have done me a fearful injury.

ROWE: Oh.

CRAWLEY: Why aren't you out on the perimeter, anyway, fighting off the Martians?

ROWE: I got lonely.

They sit down again, relax.

CRAWLEY: Here, what would you do, if the Martians was to land? Right there, on your perimeter?

ROWE: Shit myself.

CRAWLEY: That would be useful.

ROWE: Mm.

CRAWLEY: Listen, don't you think they ought to give us live ammunition?

ROWE: What for? I wouldn't know what to do with it, anyway.

CRAWLEY: Yes, but it's dangerous. I mean: what if somebody came to attack us?

ROWE: We've got our rifles.

CRAWLEY: Yes, but what are we supposed to do with them? Use them as clubs? We wouldn't stand a chance. They're pretty sharp customers, these gangs.

ROWE: Eh? What gangs?

CRAWLEY: Well I heard that the Krauts had started up some kind of resistance movement.

ROWE: What?

CRAWLEY: Straight up. They reckon that because we don't invade Russia we're not on their side.

ROWE: Oh.

CRAWLEY: They're dead right, mate. We're not.

ROWE: But surely they don't attack anybody?

CRAWLEY: Oh no? I heard they was using the old guerrilla tactics, on the British: cheese-wires, stilettoes, the lot. German Ghurkas. They cut off various parts of the body of British soldiers, just to express their disapproval for us not invading Russia.

ROWE: Ha bloody ha,

CRAWLEY: Don't you believe me? You ask Sergeant-Major West in 232 Battery – he'll tell you. He's just come fresh from H.Q., and he knows. It's a plain fact, hushed up.

ROWE: Here, I'm not going out on that perimeter wire again. I keep hearing things as it is; I'd drop dead if I had to go out there on my own thinking about that.

CRAWLEY: Well don't you think they ought to give us live ammo?

ROWE: Krauts with cheese-wires. I feel quite ill.

CRAWLEY: Oh, you'll be quite safe: all you've got to do is call for the Bombardier: he'll come to your rescue.

ROWE: Him? I'll manage, thank you. He's half daft. I can't imagine him grappling with the German Ghurkas.

CRAWLEY: **(laughs)** Here, if they wanted to cut various bits off his anatomy, they'd have a job finding them, wouldn't they? Talking about that, O'Rourke and Featherstone haven't got back from the NAAFI yet.

ROWE: He'll be lucky to see them tonight.

CRAWLEY: He will? What about us? They better bloody had come back, we're off at ten o'clock: and what time is it now?

ROWE: Quarter to.

CRAWLEY: Roll on ten – **(Pause. They sit staring at the ground.)** I'm so numb, I can't think. Do you realise it's the coldest winter for fourteen years, according to A.F.N.

ROWE: Fourteen years. 1940. Think of that, then –

CRAWLEY: Is that when fourteen years ago was? Bloody hell. That was our finest hour, wasn't it?

ROWE: I can't remember, I was only five.

CRAWLEY: You haven't changed much though, have you? Was you always afraid of the dark?

ROWE: No. It was only at night when I was younger.

CRAWLEY: Aye. Well, you'd better get back to the boundary in case the Orderly Sergeant pays one of his little calls.

ROWE: Have I got to?

CRAWLEY: Suit yourself. If you like, I'll go now and you can do the perimeter on second shift.

ROWE: At two in the morning? You win. **(Gets up.)** Don't do anything I wouldn't do.

CRAWLEY: I've got my mouth-organ to play with: what organ have you got?

ROWE: Don't be like that. See you at ten.

CRAWLEY: Roll on ten.

ROWE tiptoes off. CRAWLEY continues quietly blowing notes on the mouth-organ, as the lights come up in the hut a little, and dim on CRAWLEY. EVANS is still gazing into space, SHONE still sleeping, FLYNN smoking on the edge of his bed looking at EVANS.

FLYNN: What the hell do you sit wrapped around your stomach like that for? It's most peculiar.

EVANS: I've got a pain. Right there, in the V of the ribs.

FLYNN: Ah, everybody gets that. It's homesickness.

EVANS: I dream all day about home, but the laugh is, when I'm there I can't stand the place. I don't know what I'm doing here, nor why, nor who for, not even where I am on the map all that accurately. All I know is that I have to go home. I will even offer myself as a jumped-up eighteen-year-old joke of a Second-Lieutenant for just one chance to get home. **(Pause. FLYNN appears to be asleep.)** Sweet dreams. **(Pause. He looks at his watch and jumps.)** Christ Almighty! **(He runs to the path and looks down it, then walks into the hut and shakes SHONE, who reluctantly stirs.)** Shone! Shone!

SHONE: Stand to the guard is it?

EVANS: No, of course not. Listen. Are you awake yet?

SHONE: Hang on.

He shakes his head violently, then makes a noise like a horses which wakes up FLYNN.

FLYNN: What's going on here?

EVANS: Those two bastards haven't come back.

FLYNN: **(sitting up)** What?

SHONE: What time is it?

EVANS: It's gone quarter to ten. Almost ten to.

FLYNN: Oh Christ.

SHONE: That's just what I was going to say.

FLYNN: What are you going to do?

EVANS: I don't know. Send Shone to have a look for them.

SHONE: Why me?

EVANS: Because they hate his guts.

SHONE: Oh – well all right. Where must I look? In the NAAFI.

EVANS: I suppose so. Surely they won't have gone into town.

FLYNN: They couldn't. Sergeant Walker'd spot them going through the main guard room.

EVANS: **(to SHONE)** Try the canteen. Then try their barrack-room, it's in C. Block somewhere. Then come back. Don't hang about.

SHONE: I might have a bevvy while I'm there.

EVANS: Look, don't muck about; be back here in ten minutes, O.K. ?

SHONE: All right. Don't panic.

He pulls on his greatcoat, slowly and deliberately. While the others watch, in mounting impatience.

EVANS: Hurry up, can't you?

SHONE: Patience is a virtue. Everything comes to him who waits.

EVANS: Come on, I'm going mad here.

SHONE: I'm nearly ready. **(He does up his buttons with painful slowness, straightens his beret, and puts on his gloves, as he sings)**:

> *Little Bo-Peep Has lost her sheep*
> *And doesn't know where to find them,*
> *Leave them alone,*
> *And they will come home,*
> *Wagging their tails behind them.*
> *Ta-ta.*

He goes out. EVANS rushes to the door, and calls after him.

EVANS: You've got ten minutes – is that clear?

There is no answer. He comes back in. He and FLYNN sit down, uncomfortably aware of each other, and worried about O'ROURKE. For a while they fidget, and don't speak.

FLYNN: You'll have to charge them, Terry.

EVANS: No, **(Then, more controlled)** I mean, I won't have to. Not unless Walker turns up.

FLYNN: What's wrong with you?

EVANS: **(sharply)** I can't put anybody on a charge tonight. It's too risky.

FLYNN: **(taking this as intended to put him down)** I see, Sod you then.

EVANS: I'm sorry Bill. I didn't mean it that way.

FLYNN: I don't care which way you mean it. It doesn't worry me – you're the Bombardier.

EVANS: OK Bill, don't let's go through that again, Listen: I trust you, and I believe you. Let's leave it at that.

FLYNN: Leave it where you like, why should I worry?

EVANS: Don't be like that.

FLYNN: Like what?

EVANS: Like you are.

FLYNN: What exactly is wrong with like I am?

EVANS: Nothing, nothing, nothing.

FLYNN: Don't strain yourself. And what's all this about O'Rourke hating my guts? That's novel, I didn't think he knew I existed.

EVANS: Oh it was nothing. You're being a bit touchy, Bill.

FLYNN: Maybe, I feel touchy. But it must have been something. Now what?

EVANS: Oh, I don't know. It was Featherstone, anyway. Not O'Rourke.

FLYNN: When?

EVANS: Just now, when you were out on guard.

FLYNN: Aha. And how did I arise, so to speak, as a topic for their genteel conversation?

EVANS: Oh look – well, it was Rowe, I suppose, really, telling us about your extraordinary sexual puberty.

FLYNN: That was big of him. What did he reveal?

EVANS: Oh, just some story he said you told him about you, and some friend, and an insatiable schoolgirl. It seemed harmless enough.

FLYNN: Harmless?

EVANS: Well, you know what I mean. You never told me about it, though.

FLYNN: No, I probably thought you'd be disgusted.

EVANS: Should I be?

FLYNN: Suit yourself. It doesn't worry me. **(Pause.)** It's true of course. Every salty word of it.

EVANS: What happened to the – I mean, she got pregnant, didn't she?

FLYNN: Aborted. Legally aborted in the third month. And she never said a word. She promised to forget, and she did.

EVANS: Fantastic. You lucky bastard.

FLYNN: Lucky?

EVANS: Well, I mean. Do you ever – er – see her?

FLYNN: **(laughs)** Not often. Not in that way. Never. She moved to a new housing estate in the country, and found a timid little boyfriend. She'll probably marry him.

EVANS: And does he know –

FLYNN: I told you. She promised to forget. Last time I saw her I swear to God not a flicker of memory crossed her restless mind. She actually shook my hand, and giggled like a virgin.

EVANS: What an extraordinary thing.

FLYNN: Extraordinary? **(Smiles, looks at his watch.)** Six minutes to go. **(EVANS' mind flits temporarily back to his immediate problems.**

FLYNN now comes into the attack.) Well, tell us about your sexual experiences, then, Bombardier.

EVANS: Er – well – there's not much to tell, really.

FLYNN: You and I must go hunting together, Terry. It's better that way.

EVANS: Really?

FLYNN: I think so. **(Joking)** Then if we don't find anything, we can always amuse ourselves. Or each other.

EVANS: **(uneasy, jocular)** Featherstone said you were a pouf.

FLYNN: **(angry)** So that's what you were talking about. Why didn't you say that before, ah?

EVANS: Well – it wasn't serious.

FLYNN: **(suddenly soft again)** Ah well. Do you think I am, Terry?

EVANS: I don't know. I don't know anything really.

FLYNN: **(laughing)** Well, you're quite safe, never fear. I shan't interfere with your virginity, one way or the other. Do you believe that?

EVANS: Well yes, of course I do. Look, Bill let's forget about it, shall we?

FLYNN: Yes. That's right. Forget.

EVANS sits at the table, thinking about all that. FLYNN walks over to the door, and gazes out. CRAWLEY, downstage, plays a slow dirge to himself. FLYNN calls EVANS over. They stand side by side at the door, laughing at CRAWLEY. *The Soldier's Lament.*

EVANS: I feel sick.

FLYNN: Do you? Was it all too much for you?

EVANS: Not sick at you. Sick with fear. Is there any sign?

FLYNN: **(goes and looks up the road, comes back) Not a murmur. (Looks at his watch again.)** Three minutes.

EVANS: Crawley and Rowe won't be pleased.

FLYNN: They can like it or lump it. It's not your fault.

EVANS: Perhaps you ought to go and get them Bill. And that Shone. I'll kill that bastard.

FLYNN: Not to worry. They'll get back before Sergeant Walker pays his visit. You'll be O.K.

EVANS: He's a good bloke, Sergeant Walker.

FLYNN: He fancies himself as everybody's daddy. I don't trust him. But you can always play on his sympathy. **(Pause.)** Your mammoth moon's crept up a bit. **(Pause.)** Do you not find time the most alarming thing of all?

EVANS: This cold makes you giddy.

FLYNN: You're terrified of not being liked aren't you, Terry?

EVANS: Well – yes and no.

FLYNN: Not to worry, of course. You're on the island in a big way.

EVANS: Well – not quite, am I?

FLYNN: Mm?

EVANS: I mean, there's tonight. We're not through tonight yet.

FLYNN: Oh don't worry about that. . . .

EVANS: Oh no? Why do you think I feel so bloody nauseous? Snotty-nosed little Second-Lieutenant Pickering will be round here to turn out the guard, and there'll be nothing to turn out. They'll all be paralytic in the NAAFI.

FLYNN: Not at all. They'll be here any minute. Look, you hang on here, and I'll go and see what's happening.

CRAWLEY's voice comes complaining from off-stage.

CRAWLEY: Oi!

EVANS: Who's that?

CRAWLEY: Me, Crawley.

EVANS: What do you want?

CRAWLEY: How much longer have I got to hang around out here?

EVANS: They're on their way back.

CRAWLEY: Ha bloody ha. Here, has it gone ten?

FLYNN: **(quickly, before EVANS tells the truth)** No.

EVANS: It won't be long. Try once more round the wire.

CRAWLEY: Stroll on. **(He shambles off darkly. Stops.)** Here.

EVANS: What?

CRAWLEY: What time is it then?

FLYNN: Rot off.

CRAWLEY: I'm not talking to you, Flynn. What time is it?

EVANS: Five to ten.

CRAWLEY: I hope you're right. You wouldn't be having me on now, would you?

FLYNN: Rot off.

CRAWLEY: I'll do you, Flynn, if you say that again.

Pause. Silence. He shambles away.

EVANS: Phew!

FLYNN: Stupid bloody swede. Take no notice. Right, I'll go then.

He goes in to get his greatcoat. Another voice, ROWE's, comes from another direction.

ROWE: Oi!

EVANS: What? –

ROWE: It's ten past ten.

EVANS: So?

ROWE: So where's the relief?

EVANS: In the NAAFI.

ROWE: Oh no!

EVANS: Do you mind hanging on?

ROWE: It's bloody cold, you know.

EVANS: I know.

Pause.

ROWE: There's not much I can do, is there?

Pause.

EVANS: Thanks.

ROWE goes off gloomily. FLYNN reappears.

EVANS: Christ, where are they?

FLYNN: I'll go see.

EVANS: Thanks. And bring them back, whatever happens. Dead or alive.

FLYNN: Listen, Terry, that O'Rourke can be very unpleasant, not to say dangerous. For God's sake keep your eye on him, particularly if he's had a drop.

EVANS: Don't worry, I will.

FLYNN: And don't look so nervous.

EVANS: I'm scared stiff.

FLYNN: Don't be ridiculous. You'll get home all right. Here. **(Gives him a packet of cigarettes.)** Smoke yourself to death. I won't be long.

He goes off. EVANS, very worried, goes into the hut.

EVANS: Seventeen degrees Fahrenheit. Fifteen degrees of frost. It's mad. The

45

whole country's mad. What are we doing here anyway? Occupying the Rhine. Bloody Hell. **(He opens the tin of cigarettes that FLYNN gave him)** Christ – worms!

He is looking at them, when CRAWLEY bursts in, angry. He swings round in terror as the door opens.

CRAWLEY: Here, I just saw bloody Rowe. It's very nearly quarter past ten. What's going on then?

EVANS: **(with relief)** Crawley.

CRAWLEY: Yes, of course it's me. Who the hell did you think it was? **(It dawns on him. He points at EVANS.)** You're sitting there cacking yourself because you thought I was the Orderly Officer, aren't you? So you bloody should be. I wouldn't like to be in your sweaty boots when he gets here. Where are they, anyway, the rotten cackbags?

EVANS: I wish I knew.

CRAWLEY: They're at the rotten NAAFI, that's where they are, all of them. Where's that Flynn? He's gone as well, has he? Cheeky twit. I'll thump that get one of these days. Thinks he can get away with poxy murder well he poxy can't. Here, give us a snout.

EVANS: Look, **(giving him one)** take it out behind a truck or something. Can't you?

CRAWLEY: I'm not going out there again. What, and do O'Rourke's bash while he sits pouring Guinness down him, – not on your smelly nelly.

EVANS: Look, somebody's got to be on guard, haven't they?

CRAWLEY: Why?

EVANS: Because that's what we're here for.

CRAWLEY: And do you seriously think some daft twit of a Russian is going to creep all the way up here in the middle of the night, and tow one off to Moscow?

EVANS: **(standing up, sharply: he is not totally without command)** Crawley! When you are speaking to me, you will address me as Bombardier. You will put your heels together, and you will not give me lip. Furthermore, when you are on guard, your tour of duty continues until you are relieved: leaving your post before that time amounts to desertion. If you don't get back on guard in double time, I'll throw the lot at you, book and all. Do you hear? Right. **(Then, more naturally.)** Whatever time O'Rourke and Featherstone miss, they will make up to you on your next shift, between two and four in the morning. Don't push your luck. Now get out.

CRAWLEY: Yes, but.

EVANS: Oh rot off, can't you?

CRAWLEY: **(going)** Bloody hell . . .

SHONE staggers up to the door, pushes it open, and stumbles in. Then he stands, somewhat glazed, and stupefied.

EVANS: Well – ?

SHONE: Eh?

EVANS: You bastard. **(Goes over to him.)** You rotten, stinking parasite: I trusted you, Shone.

SHONE: I'm not jarred, I've been on the bevvy, but I'm not jarred.

EVANS: You're not jarred: what's the matter with you then? Christ, how did you manage it in a quarter of an hour? You rotten bastard. **(SHONE solemnly shakes his head, slowly and deliberately. EVANS stops.)** Here, wh – what's the matter? What is it?

SHONE: It's O'Rourke,

EVANS: What – what about him?

SHONE: He got black drunk. Anybody could have seen it coming all night. **(Passionately)** You should have seen it coming, just as much as anybody.

EVANS: **(shouts back)** Well what happened?

SHONE: They say he went berserk in his barrack-room. Then he chucked himself out of the window.

EVANS: What? Is he dead?

SHONE: Lucky for you, no. He were that drunk he fell like a sack of potatoes. Never so much as broke a bone.

EVANS: Well where is he?

SHONE: We took him back to his room to sober up. Featherstone and some of his mates are seeing to him.

EVANS: Jesus Christ. Did anybody see him?

SHONE: That's all you care about, isn't it? Can I have some cocoa?

EVANS: You'd better. **(He sits, stunned.)** Well, what am I to do? Go on, tell me, what am I supposed to do?

SHONE: I've no idea. You'd never charge him.

EVANS: Why not? It's him or me.

SHONE: Aye, I suppose it is. Well, go on then, pick up the telephone, contact the Duty Sergeant, and have him arrested. Suit yourself.

EVANS: Is it really that easy for you?

SHONE: Not a bit. I'd never charge him. But I'd never be a Bombardier. I'm putting myself in your boots. And I suppose you must, by and large.

EVANS: Did you see Flynn?

SHONE: Flynn? No, Where's he gone?

EVANS: Perhaps he'll get him here. Perhaps he'll carry the bastard here. Don't you think?

SHONE: Look, don't keep asking me. You get the extra ninepence a day, Bombardier.

EVANS: **(thinks. Then)** Oh Christ, what is O'Rourke, anyway? A stupid, drunken Irishman, – what the hell does it matter to him whether he's in a cell or out of one?

He picks up the phone to ring the Duty Sergeant.

SHONE: It's a court-martial offence, of course. Absent from guard-duty. Drunk on guard. Attempted suicide. Whichever way you look at it, he'll get eighteen months.

EVANS: Do you think so?

SHONE: Bloody certain. More likely three years.

(EVANS puts the phone down.)

EVANS: Three years?

SHONE: Could be five. Couldn't be less than eighteen months, though, could it? I mean, he's got a record as long as your arm – they couldn't give him less if they tried –

EVANS: But – Oh Jesus, I couldn't do that to any man.

SHONE prepares his bed, takes off his great-coat, B D jacket, gaiters, and finishes his fag throughout the next part of the scene, very slowly and comfortably.

SHONE: Of course, as you say, if you don't charge him and they find out, they'll charge you. You'll not get twelve months, but you can kiss your little stripe tata.

EVANS: Yes, and Blighty, and . . . well.

SHONE: And what?

EVANS: Nothing.

SHONE: You was going to say: and my little pip, weren't you? I heard they were going to send you back to Blighty to be an officer. Is that right?

EVANS: Yes, They were. They still are. Oh rot you, O'Rourke, rot you in hell. Why does he have to go showing off tonight of all nights?

SHONE: He wasn't showing off, you know.

EVANS: No? I doubt it.

SHONE: No, he wasn't. He bloody meant it.

He lies down on the bed.

EVANS: **(to himself)** I can't charge him. How could I do that?

SHONE: Can we have the light out?

EVANS: Might as well.

SHONE: Put it out for us then, Bom, I've just got settled.

EVANS reaches out and puts the light out.

EVANS: **(sarcastically)** Anything else?

SHONE: Aye, I'd like a nice fat tart with a wobbly jelly-roll and a mind like a Cairo sewer. That'd be favourite.

EVANS: You filthy-minded basket, go to sleep.

He does so, noisily. EVANS prowls around for a little, eventually sits, head in hand, fingers in his ears, with his back to the door. Then the door opens slowly, and a large bulky, breathing figure is standing there. EVANS' head is hanging limp in his hands, not noticing, hearing or seeing. Suddenly the light goes on. SHONE sits bolt upright, and EVANS turns with a jump. SERGEANT WALKER is standing there. He says, quietly, after looking at the empty beds.

SGT. WALKER: Well, Bombardier, turn out your guard.

Fade to Blackout. Curtain.

Act 2

Scene 1

The same set. They are outside the hut, with SHONE standing to attention. EVANS trembling to attention at right angles to him, and SERGEANT WALKER gravely looking on. During the following scene he never raises his voice, is calm, almost serene, and plays what he considers to be a stern, if kindly, father-figure. EVANS salutes.

EVANS: Guard ready for inspection – sah!

WALKER: You don't have to salute me lad, I'm only a sergeant, all right?

EVANS: Yessir.

WALKER: Now then, did I hear you report this guard present and correct, Bombardier?

EVANS: No sir.

WALKER: Oh really. Why not?

EVANS: I'm afraid it is not present and correct at the moment, sir.

WALKER: Oh, why is that then, Bombardier?

EVANS: **(falters, looks at SHONE, back)** Because – I don't know Sergeant.

WALKER: I see. Well maybe we can have a little chat about that in a moment or two. After we've had a look at the bit that is present and correct, eh Shone.

SHONE: Sah.

He walks in front of SHONE, and behind him.

WALKER: Gunner Shone.

SHONE: Sah!

WALKER: What exactly do you think you're on?

SHONE: S –

WALKER: Don't answer me back, boy. Tell me, Gunner Shone, are you trying to impersonate a soldier?

SHONE moves to answer yes, then stops.

SHONE: No sir.

WALKER: Sergeant.

SHONE: No, Sergeant.

WALKER: I thought maybe you weren't. Tell me what are you trying to impersonate, eh, laddie? **(SHONE is dumb.)** Right, get yourself out of here. But before you go, I've got news for you. You, Gunner Shone, are on a charge. You're on a charge for appearing on guard turn-out with your boot-laces undone. You're on another for your left gaiter, you're on another for your belt on upside-down, and you're on another for your fly-button – leave it alone, boy, leave it be. This is Germany, Shone, not the Boys' Brigade. We're here to show these bastards how to behave: right?

SHONE: Yes, Sergeant.

WALKER: Your breath smells of beer, Gunner Shone. Have you been drinking beer while on guard-duty?

SHONE: No, Sergeant.

WALKER: Has he, Bombardier?

EVANS: No, Sergeant.

WALKER: Ah well, I am very glad to hear that. Because it would have been a very serious charge indeed: drinking beer while on guard-duty is practically a hanging-charge. But now that I know you have not been drinking on guard, I suppose I'll be able to forget about it. Fall him out, Bombardier.

EVANS: **(over-shrill)** Guard – slope-arms. Guard, dis-miss.

SHONE dismisses. As he does so WALKER says firmly.

WALKER: Battery-Commander's Orders, eight-thirty sharp, Gunner. Best boots, best B. D. – smiling – understand?

SHONE: Yes Sarge.

WALKER: Right. Scarper. Bombardier.

EVANS: Sergeant?

They watch SHONE go into the hut. He instantly lies down on the bed.

WALKER: I think you and I had better have a word.

EVANS: Yes, Sergeant

WALKER: Relax, boy, relax.

EVANS: Thank you, Sergeant.

WALKER: Smoke?

EVANS: Oh thank you, Sarge.

He takes the offered cigarette, lights the Sergeant's first, carefully, then his own.

WALKER: You're very lucky it's me tonight, Bombardier Evans. Many another Sergeant I know would have had you in irons by now, turning out like that. **(Pause. No response from EVANS, beyond a gloomy nod of acknowledgement.)** You're also very lucky that I came on a little private visit of my own.

EVANS: Yes, Sarge.

WALKER: Because if I'd brought the Orderly Officer along Bombardier, your feet wouldn't have touched the ground until you were inside.

EVANS: Yes, Sarge.

Pause.

WALKER: Well, where are they? **(Pause.)** Er – before you begin. I'd just like to point out to you that I am what is known as an old soldier. I know all the gags, so you'd better let me have it straight. O.K.?

EVANS: I don't know, Sarge.

WALKER: I do, boy. Straight or nothing. Where are they?

EVANS: Well two went back to the cookhouse with the supper-cans, sergeant, and asked could they drop into the NAAFI for their fags: it's Friday.

WALKER: I see.

EVANS: And Flynn's gone to look for them.

WALKER: But the NAAFI is closed.

EVANS: Yes, Sarge.

WALKER: Some thirty-five minutes ago.

EVANS: Yes, Sarge.

WALKER: So where are they?

EVANS: Well that's why I sent Flynn to look for them, Sarge.

WALKER: Are you holding out on me son? **(Silence.)** Are you? **(Silence. FLYNN appears quietly round the corner of the hut, and watches.)** Come on, Bombardier. Your story's a load of old bullshine. Look, are you trying to cover up for somebody?

EVANS: No, Sarge.

WALKER: You'd be well advised, you know, to tell me now. Nothing will happen to you. You've got to drop somebody in it, you know, sooner or later: because if you don't, boy, they'll certainly drop you in it, and make no mistake.

EVANS: **(determined)** I'm expecting them back any minute, Sarge.

WALKER gives him a good long look. He knows exactly what is going on, and is hurt by this lack of confidence.

WALKER: Very good, Bombardier. You're a fool. You're a stupid bloody fool. And we'll leave it at that, **(FLYNN moves. WALKER swings round.)** Who goes there?

FLYNN: Me, Sarge.

WALKER: Well, where are they?

FLYNN: Just coming Sarge. They're getting some extra cocoa from the cookhouse, I believe.

FLYNN has not bothered to lie very well. WALKER looks from one to the other. He doesn't believe a word.

WALKER: Thank you, Flynn. Off you go.

FLYNN: Sarge.

He goes into the hut.

WALKER: O.K. Bombardier. You've made your bed. Now you must bloody lie in it. Next time I come around will be with the Orderly Officer, Mr. Pickering, – and by Christ, you'd better turn out that guard: fast and dressed, bulled and beautiful: and all present and correct. Because you've rejected me, Bombardier, just as you have rejected your clear line of duty. And a rejected man is a bitter enemy. Clear?

EVANS: Yes, Sarge.

WALKER: Anything to say?

EVANS: Yes, Sarge.

WALKER: What is it?

EVANS: I go to Blighty tomorrow, Sarge.

WALKER: Do you? You bloody hope you do. Fall out.

He does so. WALKER goes, abruptly, somewhat humiliated.
EVANS goes quickly in to the hut. SHONE is flat out on the bed, snoring. As EVANS comes in he does a snort and turns over. FLYNN is sitting at the table. They look at each other. EVANS sits on the end of a bed. Silence.

What happened?

FLYNN: They'll be here in ten minutes. **(Pause.)** You're mad, Terry.

EVANS: **(looking at SHONE)** Is he off? **(They listen to deep breathing, then)** Walker just put him on a charge.

FLYNN: You're joking.

EVANS: I'm not,

FLYNN: **(laughs)** The irony is sweet.

EVANS: I'm glad something pleases you. I gather I do not.

FLYNN: Ach, you make me nervous.

EVANS: Is that so?

FLYNN: Whose side do you think you're on, anyway?

EVANS: Look, Bill, I'm only standing up for your mates – you'd expect me to do the same for you, wouldn't you?

FLYNN: mates?

EVANS: Well, mine then.

FLYNN: Yours? And who the hell do you reckon to be your mates?

EVANS: Yes, but still –

FLYNN: If you imagine for one minute that either of those two rotten gobshites will think any the better of you, you're dreaming. Tell me, do you see O'Rourke embracing you with tears in his eyes and a lump in his throat, and Featherstone getting in the beer and the three of you singing and dancing round the piano – is that what you see, or what is it, because I don't understand you at all.

EVANS: Look, Bill, are you setting out to hurt me? Because if you are, I can do without it.

FLYNN: I'm not trying to hurt you, Terry, I'm trying to bring you to your senses.

EVANS: Oh, is that what you're trying to do?

FLYNN: Look, what kind of useless gesture was that you made just now? Why did you not tell Sergeant Walker exactly what was happening?

EVANS: Oh – I wish I had.

FLYNN: Ring him. Here **(He holds out the phone.)** It's not too late. He's a decent man.

EVANS: No, I can't.

FLYNN: Are you crazy? Here, let me dial the Sergeants' Mess.

EVANS: Thank you, no.

FLYNN: Ach, don't be witless.

EVANS: **(rising)** No!

Pause. FLYNN stops in mid-dial.

FLYNN: Why not?

EVANS: Because he'll charge him. He'll have to.

FLYNN: Not at all.

EVANS: Of course he will. He can't charge this one for a gaiter-strap undone, and let the others go scot-free for what amounts to deserting their post.

FLYNN: So? So what if he charges them? They deserve everything they get.

EVANS: I cannot send a man to prison for eighteen months of his life, maybe more, much more.

FLYNN: Why not? If he breaks the law, he must go to prison; and some poor bastard like you has got to send them there. Do I make myself clear?

EVANS: Yes.

FLYNN: Am I right?

EVANS: Yes.

FLYNN: Do you accept that?

EVANS: Yes.

FLYNN: So will you telephone?

EVANS: **(he shakes his head)** No. I can't.

FLYNN looks at him, motionless.

FLYNN: So you are a coward,

EVANS: Of course I'm not. What are you talking about?

FLYNN: I see. So you're a determined rebel man, is that it? You're maybe a secret revolutionary, working for Moscow behind my back, I'd never thought of that. Desperate men. Bandits all.

EVANS: Oh, don't be ridiculous, Bill, you know –

FLYNN: Well what exactly do you stand for?

EVANS: **(shouts)** Oh, leave me alone!

FLYNN: Good. Fine. Get angry. Go on, I'd love to see you get angry. I'd love to see you bursting with something.

EVANS: **(feeling weak)** What do you want me to say, Bill?

FLYNN: One thing or the other. I want you to say either God's curse on those two black bastards, I'll put them away for a lifetime, or bugger the lot of it, rot all the Bofors, I'm off to the NAAFI to join them. One or the other. Life's too short.

EVANS: I wish it was so simple. It isn't, of course, and you know it isn't.

FLYNN: Ach, you make me sick.

EVANS: I like O'Rourke.

FLYNN: Jesus!

EVANS: I've never been inside a military prison, but I can guess, and I've heard. So have you. I don't think he deserves it. I don't think he deserves to lose five years out of his life, either. It's wrong. It will do him no good. It will do him positive harm. So I am prepared to take a calculated risk on my own future. It would be much easier to report him. It would be much easier to make a 'clear-cut' decision. But I can't.

FLYNN: You're lying, Terry.

EVANS: I'm trying not to.

FLYNN: Own up.

EVANS: I'm not afraid of O'Rourke, if that's what you're thinking.

FLYNN: No, but you are afraid. It's written all over you.

EVANS: If that bloke had a decent chance, he'd be perfectly all right.

FLYNN: Crap!

Pause.

FLYNN: **(having calculated)** If you were to charge O'Rourke tonight, you wouldn't be on that train tomorrow, would you, Terry?

EVANS: I don't know. I suppose I wouldn't.

FLYNN: Too bloody right you wouldn't. You wouldn't get away for a month, with a court-martial to see to, and a serious one at that.

EVANS: If I don't go tomorrow, I don't go at all.

FLYNN: Why's that?

EVANS: I've worked it out. It wouldn't be worth their while. I've done seven months now, right?

FLYNN: Right.

EVANS: If I go now, and pass the Board, in five months' time I'll be an officer: right – right, that means a year to push; fair enough – but if I don't go now, there'll not be another place on the Board for three months, right, even assuming they still thought me suitable. Then, if I pass, another five months, then a spot of leave and a bit of waiting around and I'll be practically out of the army before they start to get their moneysworth. They'll never bother. And here I'll be, for another year and a half. I think I'd go mad.

FLYNN: You're just shit-scared, you're like a frightened little lad, who wants to run home to his mammy.

EVANS: No!

He breaks down under the strain. Then he gets up and goes out. FLYNN follows him.

FLYNN: You're quite right. It's too bloody hot in here for comfort, and I think the coke-fumes are dangerous carbon monoxide and other such secret killers abound. **(Gets up.)** Here, let me give you a hand.

They go out of the door. EVANS leans against the side of the hut.

EVANS: That's better. **(Faint noises. He smiles, ruefully.)** Sounds like it's been a great night at the NAAFI. **(He breathes in deeply, to restore oxygen to his bloodstream.)** You go in, Bill. It's bloody cold out here. I'll be all right in a second or two.

FLYNN: No, no. I'll keep an eye on you. You need someone to do that.

EVANS: **(nods)** I'm in a cold sweat, Bill.

FLYNN: Ah, of course you are. I'd be in a bit of a panic myself. Here, have a fag.

EVANS: Thanks. **(They light up.)** Look Bill, I meant what I said about O'Rourke. I don't want to send him to prison. If I don't charge him, it's not just an excuse for getting me safe home.

FLYNN: No, but it helps.

EVANS: Oh for God's sake –

FLYNN: He should be under lock and key, – for his own safety. That's all there is to it.

EVANS: Er, Bill,

FLYNN: Yes.

EVANS: You know you dropped me a packet of fags just now.

FLYNN: Mm.

He moves away, sharply, embarrassed.

EVANS: Well – it – there were. Do you know what I'm talking about, or aren't you listening?

FLYNN: I'm listening.

EVANS: Well, there were what appeared to be dead worms in it. Not fags, just worms.

FLYNN: Aha.

EVANS: Did you mean to put them in, or was it a joke?

FLYNN: **(covering up)** No. No, it wasn't a joke, I – er – I gave you the wrong tin.

EVANS: Well what do you keep those worms for?

FLYNN: Well, as a matter of fact, I fish.

EVANS: Really?

FLYNN: Yes. I fish the canal. On a Sunday afternoon.

EVANS: On your own?

FLYNN: Preferably on my own. I find it relaxing.

He more or less refuses to say any more on the subject.

EVANS: I see: that must be a nice change.

FLYNN: It is.

He goes into the hut, puts on his great-coat and re-emerges.

EVANS: Where are you going?

FLYNN: To fetch O'Rourke. It's time he was back.

He goes off, huddled up in his coat. EVANS stays, leaning against the hut. More noises of revelry. Then CRAWLEY tip-toes out of the gloom.

CRAWLEY: Oi!

EVANS: What?

CRAWLEY: Has he gone?

EVANS: Who?

CRAWLEY: That sergeant.

EVANS: What's it look like?

CRAWLEY: Right.

EVANS: Right what?

CRAWLEY: I'm coming in.

EVANS: Oh no you're not. **(In spite of EVANS trying to grab him, CRAWLEY marches in, puts down his rifle, takes off his webbing, opens his great-coat, and proceeds to warm himself at the stove throughout this next scene.)** Crawley!

CRAWLEY: Yes, Bom.

EVANS: Are you going to go on duty or are you not?

CRAWLEY: I couldn't rightly say. I'm not sure, Bom.

EVANS: Well, I'm telling you you are.

CRAWLEY: Are you, Bom?

EVANS: Yes, I bloody am.

CRAWLEY: **(peaceably)** A – a. Don't swear at me, Bom. You'll have me writing to my M. P. I've got a very sensitive ear for that kind of thing. As a matter of fact, my dad is an elder of the Bethesda chapel.

EVANS: Look, Crawley, refusing to obey an order is an offence.

CRAWLEY: Here, where's my mate O'Rourke, then? **(He looks around.)** At the cookhouse, is he? With Featherstone?

EVANS: I'm going to be obliged to charge you, if you're not very careful.

Pause. SHONE wakes up and looks at what's going on.

CRAWLEY: Was you just then talking about charging people? Evening, Shone, glad to see you're with us.

EVANS: I was talking about charging you.

CRAWLEY: And why aren't you talking about charging those other two layabouts? – It's their tour of duty, Bombardier, it's no longer mine. It ceased being mine three-quarters of an hour ago. You can't oblige me to perform their duty for them just because they're on the bevvy, mate. If you're going to charge anybody, charge them.

SHONE: Hear, hear! Them two get paralytic plastered in the rotten bloody NAAFI, miss their tour and run berserk, and I'm the poor rotten sod who gets put on a fizzer. And whose fault is that?

EVANS: Well, whose fault is it?

CRAWLEY: **(to EVANS)** Well what I say is, don't add insult to injury. I've done you a favour out of kindness, stopping out there stamping my feet up and down the perimeter, forty minutes beyond my legal entitlement: don't turn on me now, after all that, and say you're going to put me in the guard-house. Fair dos, Bom: I went out when you asked me, didn't I?

SHONE: Isn't it enough that one innocent party has been shat upon?

EVANS: Look, Crawley, it's one thing to have nobody hanging around here, – that's bad enough, tha's quite sufficient to get me busted and everybody else twenty eight days inside, – but if the Orderly Officer were to arrive and find nobody actually on guard, we'd all be inside for years. Don't you understand?

CRAWLEY: That appears to be your problem, Bombardier.

EVANS: Now look here, Crawley – **(The door has been flung open and ROWE walks in. He closes the door firmly behind him, throws his rifle with a clatter in the middle of the floor, and calmly lies down on a bed. He does not look at anybody or bother about anybody. There is a brief silence.)** Rowe, get back on duty at once. **(Silence.)** Gunner Rowe, I order you to return to your post.

Pause. Then ROWE speaks quietly.

ROWE: Rot that for a lark. I've got frost-bite.

CRAWLEY: Have you?

ROWE: Yes, I bloody have.

CRAWLEY: So have I. Where's yours?

ROWE: Then ten fingers of my hands, the ten toes of my feet, and the two cheeks of my backside. If I stay out there one minute longer, I'll have a frost-bitten cock, which I do not intend to have. I'm sorry, Bombardier I just can't help you.

There is a stunned silence. EVANS turns away and gazes at the telephone. He goes and sits at the table, and picks it up. Then he puts it down and looks at them all again. They are watching him, except ROWE, who is lying on his back, rubbing his hands. As he picks it up and begins to dial, FLYNN comes in with a cocoa thermos. He has been running. EVANS puts the phone down.

EVANS: Well? Where are they?

FLYNN: **(out of breath, nods, points)** Out there. **(He points to the thermos.)** Cocoa.

SHONE: Great, can we have it now, Bom?

EVANS: What's happening?

SHONE pours cocoa for himself, ROWE and CRAWLEY. Then for FLYNN and EVANS throughout this scene.

FLYNN: I found them where I left them, in the cookhouse. O'Rourke was vomiting Guinness and blood, fine and dandy at the cookhouse door.

CRAWLEY: Here, what's been going on then?

SHONE: That mad O'Rourke chucked himself through a window. Tried to commit suicide.

CRAWLEY: Get away.

SHONE: I tell you no lies, brother.

FLYNN: He also, at one time, had an axe. He aimed to revenge himself on the regiment by systematically chopping it up, beginning with the mascot.

CRAWLEY and SHONE: What about that? Bloody hell.

FLYNN: He no longer has the axe. But he's far from benevolent. Anyway, the main thing is that brother Featherstone is supporting him, single-handed, even now, along the dark back alleys of the camp, to this very shed. He'll be here in two minutes, I promise.

EVANS: Thank God for that.

A pause. They sit, lie or stand, thinking of O'ROURKE's great gloom, which they all understand and to some extent feel. At this moment, O'ROURKE assumes heroic stature in their minds.

SHONE: He's right desperate tonight, poor bastard.

ROWE: **(laughs softly)** Christ, I'd love to have seen him with that chopper.

FLYNN: **(quietly)** He's a maniac, and needs to be put out of his misery.

SHONE: I seen him hit the deck. He come flying through this window, twenty feet in the air, and crumpled up on the deck, like a cart-horse on ice; gentle, but definite. Thump. And I looked up, and there were these flames flickering in the window, and at first I thought it was a fire, but no – what he'd done, he'd put all his gear in a big pile on the bed, and set a match to it. Then he jumped.

CRAWLEY: Was he hurt?

SHONE: Not a scratch. Not a mark on him. Just crumpled like an overcoat. It was me picked him up, I tell you no lies.

ROWE: Was he conscious?

SHONE: He was drunk. When I shook him to see was he dead, he snorted like a pig, and then he laughed like a big, daft drunk. I think he would have fallen fast asleep, there on the deck, if I hadn't moved him – me and Featherstone.

Pause. They think about him again.

EVANS: When he gets here, he'd better go straight out on guard, – and stay out till the turn-out's over. We'll cart him away, right to the far end of the gun-park, so even if they look for him they'll never find him. I think that's the best thing. Then we're all in the clear.

CRAWLEY: It sounds to me as if he'll do what he wants, and nothing but what he wants.

SHONE: Oh, I don't know. He'll be getting a bit, you know, stupid now. He'll be sinking into a mighty stupor. He'll not give much trouble.

A noise offstage.

SHONE: Sounds like him.

EVANS: Sh!

Slowly FEATHERSTONE comes in sight, dragging the inert, blood-stained, filthy, vomit-covered carcass of O'ROURKE. The others go to the door and gaze on this sight, not moving to help. O'ROURKE mutters to himself, and bellows from time to time.

O'ROURKE: **(incoherent)** I am not going on guard, I am not going on guard, rot the Bofors, I want to rest. Rot the Bofors guns, I am not going on guard tonight.

FEATHERSTONE: Give us a hand, can't you? Don't just stand there. **(SHONE and CRAWLEY go and help him, gingerly, and together they get him into the hut, and lay him on a bed. FEATHERSTONE is sweating and half-drunk himself anyway. He sits on another bed, next to O'ROURKE, and gives in to fatigue.)** Jesus Christ Almighty, what a night. Pah! I'm covered in that rotten bastard's spew. Give us a rag, somebody.

SHONE: **(holding out cotton-waste from the waste-bin)** Here. It's a bit oily, but it'll do. Bloody hell, look at the state of him: It'll need a bit more than a bit of cotton-waste to clean him up and that's no lie. **(He goes and scrutinises**

O'ROURKE, who lies inert, mumbling.) Here, he's passed out. Eh, he's all white and quivering. I don't like the look of this: look at that, Bombardier – he looks dangerously ill to me.

EVANS: **(goes and looks at him dubiously)** Mm, Oh, I don't know, he doesn't look too bad, really.

FLYNN: **(sharply)** You should send for the M. O. right away.

FEATHERSTONE: You'll do no such thing. Over my dead body that bloody doctor walks in here.

FLYNN: Don't be so bloody stupid. He could be dying for all we know.

FEATHERSTONE: Dying of what? He was all right ten minutes ago, you saw him yourself. He was walking on his own two feet when we left the cookhouse. It's just caught up with him, that's all.

FLYNN: He could be bleeding to death from internal haemorrage for all you know – he fell from a window, didn't he?

FEATHERSTONE: He jumped.

FLYNN: Right then, so I suppose he's got to take what's coming to him?

FEATHERSTONE: **(standing up and getting hold of FLYNN's lapels)** Look, you philosophised Irish bum boy. Who asked you to open your mouth, eh? Who asked you your little opinion, eh? Can't your little friend speak for himself – can't he?

EVANS: **(trying to break it up)** All right, that'll do Featherstone. There's enough blood about the place already. Now listen, there can be no question of sending anybody for the M. O. –

FLYNN: You're mad.

EVANS ignores him. He turns away from FEATHERSTONE and sits on his bed.

EVANS: Nor can there be any question of him lying there. For your information, Featherstone, the Orderly Sergeant has already been –

SHONE: Aye, and put me on a rotten charge –

EVANS: – and he knows you've been out. He's coming back. With Mr. Pickering. When he comes back, which could be at any moment, neither you nor O'Rourke can possibly be in this guard-room. Is that quite clear?

FEATHERSTONE: You can't send him out there! He'd bloody die. He'd die of pneumonia.

EVANS: Not if we wrap him up. We can park him against a gun, out of the wind.

FEATHERSTONE: He'll die the death mate, do me a favour. Look, why can't we roll him up in a blanket, and stuff him under the bed? They'd never see him. Then you could still say he was out doing the perimeter, couldn't you?

EVANS: He has got to go out on duty.

FLYNN: And what do you do when the little Second Lieutenant insists on seeing him? Where are you then? You're both crazy, the pair of you.

FEATHERSTONE: You keep out of this, Flynn, or I'll thump you stupid.

EVANS: Listen, Bill, as long as he's out there on guard –

FLYNN: Look, if you want to get home as badly as you say you do, why are you being so naive?

EVANS: Let me do this my own way.

FLYNN: Your own way.

EVANS: **(angry)** I don't know what you are talking about.

FLYNN: Go ahead. Dig your own grave. It should be amusing to watch.

EVANS: Right. Good. Now. Let's clean him up. Featherstone, do something will you?

FEATHERSTONE: What?

EVANS: Get some of the crud off him, before it hardens. Give him a hand, will you, Rowe?

FEATHERSTONE: Oh, eh, Bom . . .

EVANS: **(firmly)** Do it.

FEATHERSTONE: Oh, bloody hell.

EVANS: Shone, go to the latrine round the back, get some water if the tap's not frozen. Quick, on the double. We can't muck about.

SHONE: What shall I fetch it in?

FLYNN: Fetch it in your Boy Scout's hat – it's your good deed for the day.

EVANS: (thrusting a mug in his hand) Here, Quick. (SHONE goes.) Bill, if you're not going to help, get out of the way.

FLYNN grins, and blows him a kiss, ironically.

FEATHERSTONE: **(making dabs at O'ROURKE)** Ugh! Bloody rotten hell. No greater love hath man than this: to wash his mate's vomit off the inside of his collar.

ROWE: **(helping him, ineffectually)** To think this rotten bastard punched me earlier on. Here, I could get my own back, couldn't I? I could spit in his ear-hole. Deafen him for life.

FEATHERSTONE: I wouldn't advise it, son, not if I was you. He's got to wake up sometime.

ROWE: I doubt it. Still. What a bloody mess –

FEATHERSTONE: Here, has he stopped breathing?

ROWE: SH! No, no such luck. Christ, look at that! Did he land on his head when he jumped out of that window?

FEATHERSTONE: He must have. **(Laughs.)** By God, he's going to have some kind of hang-over in the morning.

ROWE: **(seeing blood trickling down his sleeve, alarmed)** Eh, Bom, what about that?

EVANS: **(glances: coldly)** Yes. Wipe it up.

FLYNN: Are you aware that you could be killing him?

FEATHERSTONE: **(slowly, deliberately)** Why don't you go away, into a corner, and abuse yourself? Eh?

SHONE comes in with a mug of water, pleased.

SHONE: Here, it's warm. I made it myself.

FEATHERSTONE: You dirty bugger. You didn't?

SHONE: Of course I did. That tap got frozen up three months ago, it hasn't thawed since last October.

FEATHERSTONE: Well you can't put that on him.

SHONE: Why not? It's pure.

FEATHERSTONE: Bloody hell.

SHONE: Here, lend us your hanky.

FEATHERSTONE: Not likely. Use your own.

SHONE: All right then. Here goes. **(He dips his handkerchief in the mug, and mops the blood gently off O'ROURKE's face and forehead. The others watch him. Slowly, O'ROURKE comes round, with great oaths and groans.)** Here – it's doing the trick all right. It must be the ammonia content – do you think?

EVANS: OK, Shone, that's enough. Let him wake up.

O'ROURKE makes several violent, feverish movements, then groans and sits up, his eyes closed.

O'ROURKE: O – o – oh – A – a – ah. What's that? What's that you say? Wha-a-a-at? Don't give me none of that. Not at all! **(He opens his eyes, sees them all staring at him, and laughs wildly.)** What's up with you? What's got into you? Do I frighten you all or what is it? **(Sings jeeringly)**:

Oh I wasn't drunk and I wasn't blind
When I left my two fine legs behind
For a cannon-ball on the fifth of May
Too my two fine legs from the knees away.

He stops, looks at the effect, laughs again.

Have no fear, I am not dead, – I've bumped my bum, and I've hurt my head. How's that?

EVANS: O'Rourke, can you stand up? We've no time to lose.

O'ROURKE: **(standing up)** Oh, oh no, we have not a moment to waste, for the sheriff will arrive with his posse before we have bagged all the swag. Make haste, make haste, do not delay, for Bombardier Evans is fast on his way.

FEATHERSTONE: You fell on your head all right, didn't you?

O'ROURKE: Ah, Featherstone, my stout support, – I feel mighty unwell.

FEATHERSTONE: So you should.

O'ROURKE: I think I'll go back to sleep.

He falls back, apparently dead to the world.

SHONE: Shall I give him a shake?

EVANS: No, leave him. We'll carry him out.

FEATHERSTONE: Do what?

EVANS: Carry him.

FEATHERSTONE: You must be joking.

EVANS: I don't see why not. Here, give me a hand, Rowe – take his feet or something. **(He tries to take O'ROURKE by the shoulders.)** Right, come on.

Suddenly O'ROURKE bursts into action, sending ROWE flying one way and EVANS the other. He stands up menacingly.

O'ROURKE: Who did that? Who touched me? Don't touch me, do you hear – just don't touch me. OK – Rowe?

EVANS: Look, O'Rourke, we are trying to help you. You're in trouble, do you understand?

O'ROURKE: Oho, the laughing bombardier. How's ya bleeding heart?

EVANS: Right, that's enough. There is no time to fool around. You're to go out on guard, as far away as possible, at the top corner of the wire, and stay out of sight. If the duty-officer comes too close, that's your horrible luck, soldier. Is that clear?

O'ROURKE: I hear you, little brother.

EVANS: Good. Get your webbing on.

O'ROURKE: A – a. One moment, little brother. There is one small thing.

EVANS: **(sharp)** What?

O'ROURKE: He's quite the little man, now, isn't he? Altogether the perfect-in-every-detail pocket-size pixie.

EVANS: I'm sorry, O'Rourke, but we've got no time to waste listening to your stupid abuse. Come on now.

He goes to take O'ROURKE by the arm, but he throws him off violently, stubbornly.

O'ROURKE: Don't touch me! Now I warned you. Don't say I didn't warn you. I won't have people touching me. Pushing and pulling, with their clammy, sweaty pink hands. Is that clear now?

EVANS: You bastard, O'Rourke. You give me a pain.

O'ROURKE: A – a. Don't turn nasty. I detect a distinctly sour tone in your voice. Don't forget: you're the fellow with the helping hand.

FLYNN: **(in disgust)** You make me puke, O'Rourke. I hope you burn in hell.

O'ROURKE: Is that so? Do you really?

FLYNN: Yes I bloody do.

O'ROURKE: Aha, well I think we all know your position then, Flynn. Or do you have anything to add?

FLYNN: Nothing.

O'ROURKE: That's fine then. Your Protestant conscience is in the clear, I hope.

FLYNN: This has nothing to do with religion.

O'ROURKE: Once a Protestant, always a Protestant, Flynn. You'll die with a clear conscience, and a smirk on your justified lips.

FLYNN: Don't be childish, O'Rourke. The world has moved on beyond tired old wars like that one.

O'ROURKE: You're a clever bastard, Flynn. But if I had half a chance, I'd slit your Protestant throat, so I would.

FLYNN: It's mutual, then.

And FLYNN turns away.

EVANS: Look, O'Rourke, there's nothing for it, you've just go to go out on guard.

O'ROURKE: Aha. **(He sits, looks at EVANS. EVANS looks at the phone, O'ROURKE sees this.)** Come on then, make me.

EVANS: Don't play about, O'Rourke, I'm serious.

O'ROURKE: Shall I tell you something?

EVANS: Just say Yes or No, O'Rourke, I don't want to hear anything else.

O'ROURKE: Bombardier – for such is what you are – Bombardier, I have to inform you that you may telephone to the late King George the Sixth himself and report me, for I don't give a fart. I hope I don't shock you, but it's true.

Because, Bombardier, – for such is what you are – I happen to know that I am not long for this world.

He sits and looks at them all. FLYNN eventually laughs, a short, derisive snort.

FLYNN: Ha!

O'ROURKE: There speaks the true voice of Industrial Protestantism: cold, heartless, cynical and afraid. No wonder England's devoid of feeling: a man opens his heart to you, and all you can do is snort.

Pause.

CRAWLEY: Have you something wrong with you then O'Rourke?

No answer.

FEATHERSTONE: You've not got – something wrong, have you Danny?

O'ROURKE: Haven't I?

FEATHERSTONE: Oh why don't you talk sense, you contrary bugger?

EVANS: **(quietly)** Listen, O'Rourke, I don't know quite what you meant by all that, but I'm afraid you have to go on guard. There's been nobody out there for God knows how long, and Pickering will be here any minute: whatever happens, you can't stand there to be inspected by Pickering. Not in that state. I don't care how long you've got to live.

O'ROURKE: Do me no favours, Bombardier.

EVANS: I've done you enough already.

EVANS turns away and sits at the table. O'ROURKE looks at him, almost kindly, and decides to go. He sighs heavily.

O'ROURKE: Oh, well, come on, you. I'll need support. Thanks.

CRAWLEY and ROWE support him out. They go off-stage. EVANS picks up a rifle and hands it to SHONE.

EVANS: Here, take him that. And tell them to take him as far away from here as they possibly can. Featherstone –

FEATHERSTONE: Yes, Bom.

EVANS: Get yourself tidied up, put your webbing on and get out on watch . . .

FEATHERSTONE: Yes, Bom.

EVANS: And don't come in till I tell you. OK?

FEATHERSTONE: Yes, Bom.

He does so quickly. He is about to go.

EVANS: And keep an eye open for Pickering.

FEATHERSTONE nods and goes out of the hut. EVANS and FLYNN are alone. He collapses on a bed with relief.

EVANS: Thank God for that. **(He turns and looks at FLYNN.)** Well, Bill?

FLYNN: So far, so good.

EVANS: Oh, there's not much can go wrong now.

FLYNN: You think not?

EVANS: I hope not. Do you?

FLYNN: You're very young for your age, Terry.

EVANS: Maybe. Why do you say that?

FLYNN: Oh – well, I don't know.

EVANS: I thought it would never end.

FLYNN: Do you know something?

EVANS: What?

FLYNN: I should keep an eye on him if I were you. I've got a feeling that that bastard hasn't even begun.

EVANS despairs. FLYNN triumphs.

Blackout.

Scene 2

The same. If possible, the Bofors gun should be more in evidence. Underneath it sit FEATHERSTONE, and on the ground, propped up against a wheel, O'ROURKE, asleep. In the hut the four others quietly play cards for cigarettes. EVANS sits at the table, worrying. After a glance from FLYNN, he gets up, puts on his greatcoat, and goes out without a word.

He looks around, and on hearing FEATHERSTONE cough, he goes over to the gun, and looks in dismay at O'ROURKE.

EVANS: Wh – ?

FEATHERSTONE: **(shrugs)** He came back, Bom. Said he felt lonely on the perimeter.

EVANS: Oh no.

FEATHERSTONE: He'll never stay there you know. Not on his own.

EVANS: **(covering up his annoyance)** Well, I suppose you'd better go out there then. And I'll keep an eye on him. Do you mind?

FEATHERSTONE: Me? No. I don't mind. Makes no odds to me.

EVANS: Thanks.

As FEATHERSTONE gets up and prepares to go, SERGEANT WALKER and SECOND LIEUTENANT PICKERING appear around the hut. PICKERING is an eighteen-year-old National Service Subaltern from an ecclesiastical public school with a high voice and clear, high sense of duty.

FEATHERSTONE: **(to EVANS)** Eh, Bom – **(nods towards them.)**

EVANS: **(whispers)** Challenge them. Over there.

FEATHERSTONE steps over towards them.

FEATHERSTONE: Halt! Who goes there!

WALKER: Orderly Officer, orderly sergeant. Who's that?

FEATHERSTONE: Gunner Featherstone, sir.

WALKER: Well done, lad. Keep on your toes.

FEATHERSTONE salutes. PICKERING returns the salute.

PICKERING: Carry on,

FEATHERSTONE goes off. WALKER and PICKERING go back to the door of the hut. WALKER opens the door and goes in. They all stand up. PICKERING waits nonchalantly outside.

WALKER: **(calm)** Where's the Bombardier? Flynn?

FLYNN: Er, visiting the sentries, sergeant. He won't be long.

WALKER: Oh yes.

FLYNN: Would you like some cocoa, sergeant?

WALKER: That's very kind of you, Flynn, but I have Mr Pickering waiting outside. As the, er, Bombardier is visiting the sentries, Mr Pickering and I will have to take ourselves off to the Sergeants' Mess, to put ourselves into a better frame of mind.

FLYNN: Yes, Sergeant.

WALKER: And do put your belt on the right way up, Shone.

SHONE: Yes, Sergeant.

WALKER: All right then. Goodnight, lads.

FLYNN: Will you be back, Sarge?

WALKER: I shouldn't think so. Off the record. **(He winks.)** Goodnight.

ALL: Goodnight, Sergeant.

He goes out, talks quietly to PICKERING.

WALKER: The Guard Commander is paying a brief visit to the sentries at the moment, sir. May I recommend that we adjourn to the Sergeants' Mess?

PICKERING: Certainly, Sarnt, Delighted. **(looks at his watch.)** We will come back in fifteen minutes.

WALKER: Do you think we need to, sir?

PICKERING: **(quietly)** Of course.

WALKER: **(crestfallen)** Very good, sir.

PICKERING: **(as they go)** Tell me, Sarnt Walker, isn't the Bombardier the chap we're sending for an Officer Selection Board? . . .

They go off, leaving O'ROURKE asleep, and EVANS sitting on the Bofors. O'ROURKE begins to stir. Slowly, with great groans, he comes to. He blinks and looks around, and sits up, astonished.

O'ROURKE: Am I on guard?

EVANS: What does it feel like?

O'ROURKE: Aha. Jesus, my head. I'm so cold.

EVANS: Take a walk. Restores the circulation.

O'ROURKE: I will. Give us a hand. **(He does. O'ROURKE staggers around a bit.)** What are you going here?

EVANS: Making sure you don't die.

O'ROURKE: Damn decent of you.

EVANS: Don't mention it.

O'ROURKE: **(looking up)** The moon's very big tonight.

EVANS: I've noticed that.

O'ROURKE: Ah, but you're the noticing kind, now aren't you? Jeez, I must sit down again. My head's afloat. Here, will you shove up a bit.

EVANS: Of course.

O'ROURKE: Ah, that's better. **(They sit in silence, incongruously together. O'ROURKE puts his arm round EVANS' neck for support.)** Do you know something boy?

EVANS: What's that?

O'ROURKE: How old would you say I was, boy?

EVANS: I suppose you ought to call me Bombardier, O'Rourke.

O'ROURKE: Is that so? Now I'll tell you – you are nineteen: right?

EVANS: Eighteen.

O'ROURKE: Holy cow. Eighteen. The boy bombardier.

EVANS: Mm – hmm.

O'ROURKE: Don't umm – hmm me, boy-bombardier. I'm telling you something.

EVANS: Are you?

O'ROURKE: I am. **(Pause.)** How old would you say I was now?

EVANS: I've no idea,

O'ROURKE: Bearing in mind that I'm nothing, bearing in mind that I'm a heap of shit, and you – even you I have to lick the boots of – now what would you say my next birthday would make me?

EVANS: I've no idea. Twenty eight?

O'ROURKE: No.

EVANS: Thirty eight?

O'ROURKE: No.

EVANS: Thirty two?

O'ROURKE: Nearer.

EVANS: Oh, I give up. What is it?

O'ROURKE: What day is it?

EVANS: Friday.

O'ROURKE: And what date?

EVANS: **(pulls out watch)** Very early the eighth of February 1954.

O'ROURKE: Ah well now, isn't that something? And here I am, a big, tearsome heap of nothing, and far far from home.

EVANS: Ah, you're just moody drunk, O'Rourke, and no wonder.

O'ROURKE: Don't you hear me, boy? Don't you bombardillas hear a blind rotten word? Are you not capable?

EVANS: I was trying to be sympathetic, Danny.

O'ROURKE: Ah, get away from me with your hands across the sea and your finger up me bum.

EVANS: Look, Dan, I'm only trying to cheer you up –

O'ROURKE: Do you think better men than you haven't tried and failed, ah? Do you think you can succeed where St Francis Xavier was defeated? Ah? Go beat on your drum boy. **(Pause.)** Are you Catholic are you, or what?

EVANS: Me?

O'ROURKE: Who else?

EVANS: Well, no.

O'ROURKE: Well what are you?

EVANS: Oh, I don't know. It's very difficult to define, really, exactly where I stand.

O'ROURKE: Aha. **(Smiles.)** But you do your best for God, like?

EVANS: No, I – well, as I was –

O'ROURKE: I hate Him.

EVANS: God?

O'ROURKE: Who else?

EVANS: Well that seems hardly – well, I mean, if you hate Him, you must believe in Him. And if you believe in Him, surely you have to accept his goodness. Well, you can hardly hate that.

O'ROURKE: I hate all goodness, boy, particularly divine.

EVANS: Surely – ah well, I suppose you know your own mind.

O'ROURKE: I do.

Pause.

EVANS: And is that why you – took the leap, so to speak?

O'ROURKE: What? Because of God? Because of the Almighty is it? Jesus, boy, you're adrift.

EVANS: Well, I didn't mean that literally, but is that what's at the root of the problem?

O'ROURKE: The root . . . The root of the problem . . . **(He broods, with heavy irony.)** Do you know Lance-Bombardier, I honestly don't think it is. No.

EVANS: Oh.

Pause.

O'ROURKE: I suppose you're stuck now. Stumped is it?

EVANS: Well, I mean, it's not really up to me to pry into these things is it? Anyway, I'm off to England – tomorrow – so it makes no odds to me, either way.

O'ROURKE: It would if I tried again. Wouldn't it? **(Laughs.)** By Christ. Yes, it would. I might be dead, but you'd be in the mire, wouldn't you? **(Laughs.)**

EVANS: Would you try again?

O'ROURKE: Aha, I have you worried now, my beauty.

EVANS: I'm not worried for my sake – but –

O'ROURKE: Of course you are. What odds does it make to you whether I'm alive or dead? You said so yourself – none at all. In fact, I think you'd prefer me dead. You find me an embarrassment, don't you?

EVANS: Of course I wouldn't prefer you dead –

O'ROURKE: I worry you don't I?

EVANS: Of course you do, but –

O'ROURKE: Of course – I might not decide however, to go it alone: had you thought of that?

EVANS: What do you mean?

O'ROURKE: **(looks at him)** I mean, if I was to stick this bayonet in you, my prime young Lance-Bombardier, first – I could take you with me, as it were. A kind of clean sweep: don't you think?

EVANS: I don't think you would Dan.

O'ROURKE: Oh really? You don't think it would give me great pleasure to put an end to your pathetic existence? You don't think I owe it to the world as my final and only contribution to progress?

EVANS: Oh come off it, Danny.

O'ROURKE: **(sharp)** Call me O'Rourke. Call me Gunner O'Rourke, Lance-Bombardier. Even a heap of shit can be called by its rightful name,

EVANS: Ah, now, Dan.

O'ROURKE: You heard me. **(He reaches for his rifle.)**

EVANS: Put that bayonet away, Dan. **(O'ROURKE fixes the bayonet on the end of the rifle with a sharp click, and looks at EVANS. He is tormenting him because he genuinely despises him.)** Now listen to me, O'Rourke.

O'ROURKE: That's better. That's a lot better, Lance Bombardier. Now then – **(he waves the rifle vaguely)**; what do you think, what would you say was the reason I took the leap, as you call it? Come ahead, speak up now.

EVANS: Well, I've really no idea. Perhaps some marital problem. I mean, it's normally something to do with people's private life isn't it?

O'ROURKE: Is that so?

EVANS: I don't even know if you're married or not.

O'ROURKE: I'm thirty, not eighty – I've slept with every class of tart from Siberians to Polynesians, had them all, no bother at all. I don't need a wife – I hire one by the hour.

EVANS: Do you?

O'ROURKE: I do son. No wife, no marital problem. So you're wrong. Try again.

EVANS: Why do you want me to go through this?

O'ROURKE: It passes the time.

EVANS: You do know, I hope, that I could have had you charged already on about six or eight counts, not including threatening me with that bayonet.

O'ROURKE: Come on – guess.

EVANS: Guess what?

O'ROURKE: Come on. For the sport. Why? Think why?

EVANS: I don't know why. You could have had syphilis of the third degree for all I know.

O'ROURKE: Wrong. A good try, but wrong. No clap, no chancres, no syphilis: I have never suffered from pox of any description. I always take extreme care not to. Guess on.

EVANS: Oh, for God's sake, this is stupid, Look, O'Rourke, I'm doing you a favour.

O'ROURKE: Do me no favours kiddy.

EVANS: Look, you have left your post, got drunk on guard, you've attempted suicide, broken windows, vomited on your best battledress, and threatened me with a bayonet. You've dropped me in it, right, left and centre, with Sergeant Walker, and with Crawley and Rowe, and probably with the Orderly Officer when he turns up. And still I haven't charged you.

O'ROURKE: Ah, rot off.

EVANS: Let's get this clear, O'Rourke. I am doing you a favour.

O'ROURKE: I said do me no favours. If you want to, report away. I couldn't give a monkey's fart.

EVANS: You don't know what you're saying. You don't know what you're talking about.

O'ROURKE: Oh yes I do, kiddy. Oh yes, I do, I've been there, many a time. How often have you?

EVANS: And you want to go back? For three years?

O'ROURKE: Nobody pities me, Bombardier. Forget it.

EVANS: Oh, come on, now, Dan –

O'ROURKE: **(mimicking)** Oh, come on, now, Dan – you know why you won't report me, don't you? Because if you report me, you've crapped it, haven't you? You've failed to keep a grip on your little guard haven't you, and you have blotted your copy book, and you won't be sent to Blighty for an officer after all, you'll have to stay out here, like all of us poor bastards, until January nineteen fifty rotten six. Won't you? You don't feel sorry for me – you're just making a mess in your trousers in case they find out about you.

Pause.

EVANS: **(quietly)** That's not the whole truth Danny.

O'ROURKE: **(laughs)** But the thought had crossed your mind maybe? **(He looks at EVANS, almost with sympathy.)** I told you I was a sergeant once did I?

EVANS: I think so.

O'ROURKE: **(smiles)** It didn't last long. I got three years for looting in Palestine. And then three months for incorrect dress at the Battle of Imchon in Korea. My flies were undone on morning parade, and the officer didn't like me. We fought the battle, then I got charged. I hoped the bastard would get shot, but the Chinese are notoriously cross-eyed when it comes to marksmanship. Then three months in Gravesend for drunk and disorderly. Then six months in Moascar, for thumping an Egyptian – apparently the one I chose to thump was one of ours. And now?

EVANS: I think you've done enough.

O'ROURKE: **(laughs viciously, sudden change of tone)** So guess.

EVANS: Guess what?

O'ROURKE: Guess why – why, why, why – go on.

EVANS: I've no idea.

O'ROURKE: Think of something. Anything.

EVANS: Oh.

O'ROURKE: Go on. Pass the time.

EVANS: I don't know. Money. Do you owe money?

O'ROURKE: No. Again.

EVANS: Well – perhaps somebody died – mother, girl –

O'ROURKE: No, No, No.

Pause.

EVANS: I know. Is it – **(Pause.)** Have you got cancer? **(O'ROURKE laughs violently.)** No? **(O'ROURKE shakes his head, still laughing.)** Some other disease?

O'ROURKE: No. **(still laughing.)** No disease.

EVANS: **(shouts)** Well, what then? I've no bloody idea why you wanted to jump out of your rotten window. And I don't bloody well care.

Silence.

O'ROURKE: **(quietly)** No. I don't think you do.

At that moment, SERGEANT WALKER and SECOND LIEUTENANT PICKERING come round the corner again. WALKER belts on the door of the hut, throws it open and, standing outside, shouts:

WALKER: Stand to the guard! **(The four SOLDIERS grab rifles, berets etc., and turn out smartly and quickly, and stand to attention in a line.)** Where's the Bombardier? Flynn?

FLYNN: Still visiting the sentries, sah!

WALKER: **(shouts)** Bombardier! Bombardier Evans! Bombardier Evans!

PICKERING stands casually tapping his leg with his cane swagger-stick, looking very relaxed.

O'ROURKE: Away wit' ya, little manny, can't ya hear ya Daddy callin' ya home?

EVANS: Don't you move, O'Rourke – got that? Don't you bloody well move. And for Chrissake don't puke.

O'ROURKE: Away to your Da.

EVANS: Coming Sergeant. **(He trots over to the guard, and stands in his position at the head. He takes a sharp, military step forward and says:)** Guard present and correct, sah!

As PICKERING and WALKER silently, solemnly inspect the guard, and then dismiss them and remain talking to EVANS in the background, quietly, O'ROURKE speaks downstage.

O'ROURKE: For Chrissake don't puke. It's not possible. **(He gets up and walks around, laughing. Then he stops and looks at the bayonet, which is still on the end of the rifle.)** Pig-sticker! Give me time. Give me time. **(He looks over to the guard inspection.)** You bastards won't, will you? You bastards won't give me time to scratch me bum.

While the Guard Inspection goes on, O'ROURKE very efficiently takes off his greatcoat, battledress top, puts them neatly in a pile, counts his money, puts his cigarettes on the side of the gun, and picks up the rifle and bayonet.

The Inspection, quick and perfunctory, is over. EVANS dismisses the guard.

EVANS: Guard dis – miss!

They dismiss. As they go into the hut.

PICKERING: Now I want to inspect your sentries Bombardier. Where are they?

EVANS: Oh – over that way sir.

PICKERING: Lead on, Bombardier. Who are they?

EVANS: Oh, er – Featherstone, sir, and O'Rourke.

PICKERING: Yes, I want to see them.

EVANS leads PICKERING and WALKER away in the opposite direction from O'ROURKE, who is watching this with interest. The others are in the hut. They turn out the light and lie on the bed. O'ROURKE turns to the audience.

O'ROURKE: The Bofors gun, sirs, is a mighty fine thing. It is primarily a light anti-aircraft gun, designed – beautifully designed, you will agree – for the role of protecting infantry in the field and forward headquarters of all kinds from low-flying enemy aircraft. You have have observed what we call the magazine, into which we slip the little shells, four at a time. By Jove, sirs, when she fires one single shot, 'tis thunder, but when she challenges the strafing attacker on non-stop repeat, oho, sirs, she bucks and sweats and strains with joy, and delivers herself of thirty-two great little rounds per minute, belittling the thunder, and deafening the very welkin itself. You may have observed also, sirs, the two grand little seats, where the operators operate. One finds the height, his butty the angle, and do you know, sirs, that in the latest model of all, they say that one man does both, with the aid of electrical assistance. It is indeed a fine gun, the Bofors light ack-ack. It has been, of course, obsolete since 1942, the year it was put on the market, and even the ultimate in Bofors guns has no particular role to play in the event of genuine war, with its nuclear fission. Even, need I say it, in the event of a more conventional conflict, it will be found to be very rarely in the same spot as the more mobile aircraft of today, and even it it were, they are too fast, and too small, to present a suitable target. It is an inefficient and obsolete weapon, sirs, of which our Army has many thousands: and you have, in your wisdom, asked me, Gunner O'Rourke, to guard it with my life, thinking that, as my thirtieth year looms up to strike me between the eyes, I would indeed do anything, anything, to preserve and shelter from all Bolshevik harm, a thing so beautifully useless, so poignantly past it, so wistfully outdated, as my youth, or a Bofors gun. I would, and I shall, lay down my life for it. I have tried already, and failed. Here, in the sacred presence of the Bofors gun, I can only succeed.

He sets the rifle and bayonet up against the wheel of the gun, and is about to drop onto it, when PICKERING, WALKER and EVANS reappear by the hut.

PICKERING: I insist on finding him, Bombardier. Is that absolutely clear?

EVANS: Yes, sir.

PICKERING: Right. We'll spread out. You go that way, Sergeant Walker that way, and I'll go this way.

They spread out, WALKER and PICKERING going off again, leaving EVANS at the hut. O'ROURKE falls onto the bayonet during PICKERING'S last line. EVANS hurries over to the gun. He finds O'ROURKE on his face, and thinks he is asleep.

EVANS: Wake up For God's sake, wake up, O'Rourke look **(He turns him over and**

sees blood all over his stomach.) Oh. **(He bites, his lip, not knowing what to do. He tries to find out if O'ROURKE is still alive. Then a long pause as he realises that he is dead. He gets up slowly. A wild rage comes over.)** You bastard. You – **(He kicks him.)** You vicious bastard. I'll get you for this. You're on a charge. **(Kneels down, whispers.)** Do you hear that – you're on a fizzer – All right? Battery Commander's orders, eight thirty in the morning, best boots, best B.D. – smiling, understand?

SERGEANT WALKER comes back to the hut.

WALKER: Bombardier! Bombardier Evans!

EVANS: You didn't have to do this to me, did you? You wanted to. You wanted to.

WALKER: **(coming over)** Bombardier! **(He sees EVANS kneeling beside O'ROURKE.)** Is that him? Is he drunk, boy? If he's passed out, you're for it boy. **(He then sees O'ROURKE is dead.)** Holy Jesus!

EVANS: W – will I get to Blighty tomorrow, do you think, Sarge?

WALKER: Is that all you can say?

EVANS: Don't – don't shout at me just yet, Sarge. I can't think of anything else. I mean – what else is there?

WALKER: Is he dead?

EVANS: Yes.

Pause.

WALKER: You won't be going home, you know. Not for donkey's years. **(Loud.)** Sah! Mr Pickering sah! We have found Gunner O'Rourke! **(To EVANS.)** Stand up, Bombardier. That's it, lad, stand to attention, here comes the Orderly Officer. Now then, Stand at – ease! Atten – shun! As you were – shun! As you were – shun! As you were – shun! **(As the curtain begins to come down, PICKERING appears.)** Bombardier Evans, sir, and Gunner O'Rourke. **(To EVANS)** Saluting! To the front – salute! **(EVANS salutes.)** Mark – time! **(He marks time, saluting, like a pantomine chorus, as PICKERING looks sharply at WALKER, and WALKER indicates the body.)** Gunner O'Rourke, sir.

End of Play